The Rocky Mountain
sweet shoppe cookbook

Culinary Sensations For the Sweet Tooth

Recipes: Patty Ross

Set Design: Amy Larson

Published by Not Home Yet Publishing, Littleton, CO

For general information on our other products and services, to obtain technical
support, or to place book orders, please contact our Customer Care Department within
the U.S. at (303) 972-0895.

Library of Congress Cataloging-in-Publication Data:

The Rocky Mountain Sweet Shoppe Cookbook / Not Home Yet Editors.

Includes index.
ISBN 978-0-615-21258-6
Printed in China by Everbest through Four Colour Imports, Ltd.

NotHomeYetPublishing
Laugh ... Learn ... Lend a Hand

This Cookbook is Dedicated to
the Spirit of Giving
. . . and the Old Adage that . . .
"Food is Love".

Definitions

Favorite

Recipe is an Editor's Favorite; Highly Recommended.

Quick n' Easy

Preparation Time Less than 30 Minutes.

Low Sugar

Recipe with Low or No Sugar.

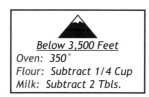

Below 3,500 Feet
Oven: 350°
Flour: Subtract 1/4 Cup
Milk: Subtract 2 Tbls.

Adjustments to Be Made to the Recipe if You Live Below 3,500 Feet in Altitude.

4

Table of Contents

Friends Who Bake Together, Stay Together ...

Choose a cold weather day during the Holiday Season,
or a vacation day during the Summer,
and invite a friend over to do some baking
and candy making.
You'll be cooking up memories that
last a life time!

The Candy Shoppe

We're delighted to offer this delectable selection of
Caramels, Hard Candies, Divinity, Toffees and
Chocolate Covered Fondant Centers of all varieties.
First-Class Candymaking is easy and fun, with the
proper tools and techniques (see page 237).

Best of the West Toffee

The Candy Shoppe

2 Pounds Toffee

√ Favorite

This classic old time favorite is surprisingly easy to make.

1 1/2 Cups Slivered Almonds
1 1/2 Cups Soft Butter
2 Cups Sugar
1/4 Cup Light Corn Syrup
1/4 Cup Water
2 Cups Milk Chocolate Chips
2 Cups Finely Chopped Pecans, Lightly Toasted

tip

To line a pan with foil without tearing it, invert the pan and shape the foil over the bottom. Lift the shaped foil off, and fit it into the upright pan, pressing it gently into the corners (see page 238).

tip

Perform the candy thermometer test on page 246 to determine the proper cooking temperature at your altitude.

Caution

Watch mixture closely; it will easily burn near the 300˚ mark.

Variation

Substitute walnuts for the pecans, and semi-sweet chocolate for the milk chocolate.

1. Arrange almonds and whole pecans (separated) in a single layer on a foil-lined baking sheet in a 350˚ oven for 7-8 minutes, stirring occasionally until light golden brown. Cool completely. Use a nut mill to finely chop pecans. Line a 10 x 15 x 1 inch jelly roll pan with foil. Grease with butter and set aside.

2. Melt butter in a heavy 3 quart saucepan over medium heat. Add sugar, corn syrup and water. Stir with a wooden spoon, and cook over medium high heat, stirring constantly, until mixture comes to a boil. Reduce heat to medium, and boil, without stirring, to 300˚ (hard-crack stage).

3. Immediately remove from heat and stir in almonds. Pour mixture into prepared pan, spreading to outer edges. Immediately sprinkle chocolate chips evenly over candy. Let stand 5 minutes, or until chocolate becomes shiny. Use a knife to spread melted chocolate evenly over toffee. Immediately sprinkle with chopped pecans. Compress mixture with a spatula, so pecans adhere to chocolate. As candy begins to set (about 3-5 minutes), use a cleaver or heavy duty knife to score into desired sized pieces. Allow candy to cool and set (about 2 hours).

4. Do NOT cover the candy until the chocolate has set and dried. Store between sheets of wax paper in an airtight tin, plastic craft container with lid, or foil covered container. Keep in the refrigerator for up to 4 weeks. Do not freeze or store at room temperature.

This super easy toffee contains only 4 ingredients.
All 3 variations have an unbeatable taste!

1. Line an 10 x 15 x 1 inch jelly roll pan with foil leaving a 2-inch overhang on 2 sides. Grease with butter and set aside. Toast pecans and cool completely.

2. Butter the insides of a 4 quart heavy saucepan. Melt the butter and water over medium heat. Turn heat to high, add sugar, and stir with a wooden spoon until mixture comes to a boil. If sugar crystals are present, wipe down with a damp paper towel. Immediately add almonds, and turn heat down to medium high. Stir constantly until the nuts turn golden brown, or about 286° (soft-crack stage; about 15 minutes). Mixture will also have turned a deep brown caramel color.

3. Immediately pour into prepared pan, and let candy stand at room temperature for 15 minutes. Use a sharp edge to deeply score candy in the pan, into 75 (1 by 2 inch) pieces (15 rows by 5 rows). Wait 5 minutes and score again. When candy is cooled, it will break along score lines.

4. Melt chocolate in a 1 quart oven proof saucepan using the oven method described on page 245. Dip desired number of candies into chocolate, making sure to coat entire piece. Shake off excess, and roll desired number of pieces in nuts. Place on waxed paper lined baking sheets to cool and set (about 2 hours).

5. Do NOT cover the candy until the chocolate has set and dried. Store between sheets of wax paper in an airtight tin, plastic craft container with lid, or foil covered container. Keep in the refrigerator for up to 4 weeks. Do not freeze or store at room temperature.

2 Cups Soft Butter
2/3 Cup Water
2 Cups Sugar
2 Cups Whole Raw Almonds

<u>Chocolate and Nut Coating:</u>
16 oz. Milk Chocolate
2 1/2 Cups Finely Chopped
    Toasted Pecans

tip

Perform the candy thermometer test on page 246 to determine the proper cooking temperature at your altitude.

tip

To save time, purchase the pecans already finely chopped. To toast, arrange in a single layer on a foil lined baking sheet in a 350° oven for 5-8 minutes, stirring twice, until golden brown.

Caution
Be careful, mixture will splatter while boiling. Do not over cook; candy will smoke and burn easily.

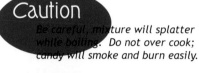

Colorado Caramels

The Candy Shoppe

49 Caramels

✓ Favorite   Quick n' Easy

These caramels are so creamy and so easy;
make them ahead of time to have on hand.

1 Cup Light Corn Syrup
8 oz. Sweetened Condensed
    Milk
3/4 Cup Milk
1/2 Cup Heavy Whipping
    Cream
1/2 Cup Soft Butter
2 Cups Sugar
1 Tsp. Vanilla

Foil or Wax Paper Squares w/
    Ties (Optional)
Mini Candy Cups (Optional)

1. Line a 9-inch square pan with foil leaving a 2-inch overhang on 2 sides. Generously grease with butter and set aside.

2. In a heavy 3 quart saucepan, combine corn syrup, condensed milk, milk, whipping cream, butter and sugar. Cook over medium heat, and stir occasionally with a wooden spoon, until mixture comes to a boil. If sugar crystals are present on inside of pan, wipe down with a damp paper towel.

3. Cook, stirring constantly, to 240° (soft-ball stage; about 26-28 minutes). Remove from heat. Stir in vanilla. Immediately pour mixture, without stirring or scraping, into prepared pan. Let sit, uncovered, at room temperature overnight.

4. Remove caramels from pan using foil edges to lift. Transfer to a flat cutting surface and use a cleaver or heavy duty knife to cut into 49 pieces (7 rows by 7 rows). For gift giving, wrap in foil or wax paper squares, or serve in mini candy cups.

5. Caramels stay fresher if left uncut until served (cover pan tightly with foil until ready to cut). Caramels can be individually wrapped in wax paper or plastic food wrap, and stored in an airtight container in a cool, dry place at room temperature for up to 2 weeks. For best results, do not store in the refrigerator or freezer.

tip

To toast pecans, arrange whole nuts in a single layer on a foil-lined baking sheet in a 350° oven for 8-10 minutes, stirring 2 or 3 times until desired flavor is reached. Cool completely, then use a chef's knife and cutting board to coarsely chop (see page 240).

tip

Perform the candy thermometer test on page 246 to determine the proper cooking temperature at your altitude.

Caution

Do not cut caramels until they have set at least 24 hours. They will be too sticky.

Variation

Add 1 cup of your favorite chopped nuts to the mixture with the vanilla, or coat the caramels with milk chocolate.

Favorite

This soft taffy combines the flavors of butterscotch and chocolate in a chewy layered candy.

1. Line an 8-inch square pan with foil, leaving a 2-inch overhang on 2 sides. Grease with butter and set aside. Place chips separately in 2 small microwave safe bowls.

2. In a heavy 3 quart saucepan, combine butter, marshmallows, half n' half and salt. Cook and stir with a wooden spoon, over medium low heat until smooth. Remove from heat. Meanwhile, microwave each bowl of chips 1 minute 30 seconds at 70% power, or until melted and smooth. Pour half of the marshmallow mixture into one of the bowls with melted chips. Gently stir the mixture until creamy and smooth. Pour the other melted chip mixture into the pan with the remaining marshmallow mixture. Gently stir the mixture until creamy and smooth.

3. Pour the butterscotch mixture into the prepared pan. Spread the chocolate mixture over the butterscotch. Use a spreader if necessary, to carefully level out mixture in pan. Cool at room temperature about 1 hour, then chill 2 hours.

4. Remove taffy from pan using foil edges to lift. Transfer to a flat cutting surface and use a sharp edge to cut into 48 rectangular pieces (8 rows by 6 rows).

5. Wrap taffy pieces individually in wax paper squares (see photo). Store in an airtight container at room temperature for 1 week, or in the refrigerator up to 3 weeks. Do not freeze.

1/2 Cup Soft Butter
60 Large Marshmallows
3 Tbls. Half n' Half
1/2 Tsp. Salt
1 Cup Butterscotch Flavored
  Chips
1 Cup Semisweet Chocolate
  Chips

Wax Paper Squares

tip
Using half n' half is the secret to this creamy taffy. You can substitute 2% Milk.

Variation
Make just one flavor taffy by using 2 cups of a single flavor chip, instead of 1 cup each flavor.

Chocolate lovers prepare yourselves - -
this chewy candy is sure to please!

1/4 Cup Soft Butter
3/4 Cup Light Corn Syrup
1/4 Cup Cold Water
1 1/2 Cups Sugar
4 oz. Semisweet Baking
    Chocolate
1/2 Tsp. Salt
1 Cup Half n' Half
2 Tsp. Vanilla
1 Cup Chopped Toasted
    Walnuts

tip

When cooking candy, always place the liquids in the pan first. This will eliminate sugar crystals from forming on the sides of the cooking pan.

tip

To measure corn syrup, spray the inside of the measuring cup with nonstick cooking spray, so the syrup will slide right out and not stick to the cup.

1. To toast walnuts, place whole nuts in a single layer on a foil-lined baking sheet in a 350˚ oven for 8-10 minutes, stirring 2 or 3 times, until desired flavor is reached. Cool completely, then chop with a chef's knife on a cutting board.

2. Line an 8-inch square pan with foil leaving a 2 inch overhang. Grease with butter. Butter the insides of a heavy 2 quart saucepan. Combine butter, corn syrup, water, sugar, chocolate and salt in saucepan. Cook and stir with a wooden spoon over medium heat, until smooth and blended. Gradually add half n' half. Cook and stir until mixture comes to a boil.

3. Cook over medium heat, stirring occasionally, until candy thermometer reaches 242˚ (firm-ball stage; about 30 minutes). Remove from heat, and stir in vanilla and walnuts. Immediately pour into prepared pan. Cool for 1 hour. Lift candy from pan using foil edges to lift. Transfer to a flat cutting surface. Remove foil and use a cleaver or heavy duty knife to cut into 48 candies (8 rows by 6 rows). If candy sticks to the cleaver or knife, spray it with nonstick cooking spray.

4. Store between sheets of wax paper in an airtight container in the refrigerator for up to 1 month. To freeze, wrap cut pieces in plastic food wrap, and freeze for up to 6 months. Do not store at room temperature; however, candy is best served at room temperature.

Caution

Perform the candy thermometer test on page 246 to determine the proper cooking temperature at your altitude.

Variation

Peanuts are an excellent substitution for the nuts in this recipe.

√
Favorite

*Without a doubt, our favorite caramel dipped candy;
marshmallows, peanuts and chocolate round out the ingredients.*

1. To finely chop peanuts, use a mini chopper (see page 240). Place in a shallow bowl. Use kitchen shears to cut each marshmallow in half. Set aside.

2. Place caramels and half n' half in a small sized microwave safe bowl. Microwave on HIGH 2 minutes and 15 seconds, stirring every 60 seconds. Mixture will be runny.

3. Insert a toothpick into each marshmallow half. Immediately dip into caramel until evenly coated, then use a spoon to coat evenly with nuts. Set on wax or parchment paper lined baking sheet to set up (about 30 minutes).

4. Melt chocolate in a 1 quart oven proof saucepan using the oven method described on page 245. Remove toothpicks from candies, shake off excess peanut coating, and dip into melted chocolate to coat evenly. Place on prepared baking sheet to set (about 2 hours).

5. Do NOT cover the candies until the chocolate has set and dried. Store between sheets of wax paper in an airtight tin, plastic craft container with lid, cardboard box with lid, or foil covered container. Keep in a cool, dry, dark place (i.e. closed kitchen cabinet), for up to 4 weeks. Do not refrigerate or freeze.

1 (14 oz.) Bag Caramels
1/4 Cup Half n' Half
2 1/2 Cups Finely Chopped
    Cocktail or Dry Roasted
    Peanuts
24 Large Marshmallows
16 oz. Milk Chocolate
Wooden Toothpicks

tip

For test purposes, we used Kraft Brand Caramels and Hershey's Brand 8 oz. Chocolate Bars. Fresh marshmallows work best.

This heavenly divinity is light and fluffy, and full of Christmas cheer! It's best to wait for a dry weather day, as humidity can affect the texture.

✓ Favorite

2 Egg Whites, at Room Temperature
1/2 Tsp. Salt
2 1/2 Cups Sugar
2/3 Cup Water
1/2 Cup Light Corn Syrup
5 Drops Green Food Coloring
1 Tsp. Vanilla
1/2 Cup Chopped Walnuts
1/3 Cup Red and Green Candy Coated Milk Chocolate Pieces (We Used M&M's Brand)

tip

Remove eggs from the refrigerator 20-30 minutes before candy making. Remember, eggs separate more easily when they are COLD.

tip

Perform the candy thermometer test on page 246 to determine the proper cooking temperature at your altitude.

Variation

Substitute miniature chocolate chips and chopped candied cherries, for the walnuts and candy pieces.

Caution

Do not over beat; candy will become grainy. We recommend you use a minute timer with this recipe (see page 241).

1. Line a baking sheet with wax or parchment paper and set aside.

2. In a large mixing bowl, beat the egg whites and salt. When soft peaks form, set aside. Combine the sugar, water and corn syrup in a 2 quart heavy saucepan. Cook over medium heat, and stir with a wooden spoon, until sugar is completely dissolved and the mixture comes to a boil. If sugar crystals are present on inside of pan, with down with a damp paper towel.

3. Increase heat to medium high, and cook, without stirring, until the mixture reaches 260° (hard-ball stage; about 7-8 minutes). Immediately remove pan from heat. Re-beat the egg whites for a few seconds to reincorporate any separation. With the beater running at high speed, slowly and carefully pour the hot syrup into the egg whites in a thin, steady stream. Beat until the divinity begins to lose its sheen (about 30 seconds). Stop the mixer, scrape sides of bowl, add food color and vanilla, and continue to beat, until mixture holds its shape when dropped from a spoon (about 8 minutes).

4. Gently fold in walnuts and candies. Stir just until combined. Drop mixture by tablespoonfuls onto prepared baking sheet. Let set (about 20 minutes).

5. Store between sheets of wax paper in an airtight container, in a cool, dry place at room temperature for up to 10 days. Do not refrigerate or freeze.

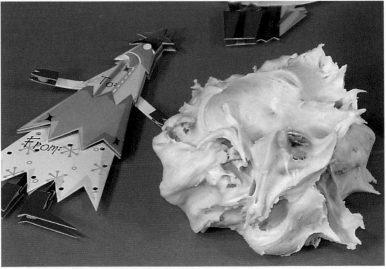

5 Pounds

✓ Favorite

Quick n' Easy

Ralphie's Rocky Road Candy

When folks try this delectable candy,
they always request the recipe!

1. Heat oven to 350°. Place whole almonds in single layer on a foil-lined baking sheet in oven for 8-10 minutes, turning after 4 minutes. Test for crispness, but be careful; nuts are HOT! Remove from oven and cool completely.

2. Line a 10 x 15 x 2" baking pan with foil, leaving a 2 inch overhang on 2 opposite sides. Spray with nonstick cooking spray and set aside. Melt the chocolate in a 4 quart oven proof saucepan using the oven method described on page 245.

3. Remove chocolate from oven. Let cool 2-3 minutes. Gently stir in nuts and marshmallows, just until coated and combined. Immediately pour mixture into prepared pan and use a large spoon to evenly spread to all edges.

4. Let candy set (about 2 hours). Remove candy from pan, using foil edges to lift. Transfer to a flat cutting surface and use a cleaver or heavy duty knife to cut into 2 inch square pieces.

5. Do NOT cover the candy until the chocolate has set and dried. Store between sheets of wax paper in an airtight tin, plastic craft container with lid, cardboard box with lid, or foil covered container. Keep in a cool, dry, dark place (i.e. closed kitchen cabinet), for up to 4 weeks. Do not refrigerate or freeze.

60 oz. Milk Chocolate
10 1/2 oz. Bag Miniature
  Marshmallows
2 1/2 Cups Whole Almonds,
  Toasted

tip

For testing purposes, we used 8 oz. sized Hershey's Brand Chocolate Bars.

Caution

Do NOT refrigerate chocolate. It will discolor or lump if exposed to any moisture.

2 Dozen Caramel Patties

✓
Favorite

This candy shoppe favorite contains only 4 ingredients;
the result is creamy peanut caramel surrounded by white chocolate.

1 (14 oz.) Bag Caramels
1 Tbls. Half n' Half
2 Cups Cocktail or Dry Roasted
   Peanuts
12 oz. White Chocolate

tip

For test purposes, we used Kraft Brand Caramels, and Ghiradelli Brand Premium White Chocolate.

1. Line a baking sheet with parchment paper and set aside. Combine caramels and half n' half in a medium sized microwave safe bowl. Microwave on HIGH 2 minutes and 15 seconds, stirring every 60 seconds, until smooth and creamy.

2. Stir in peanuts, and mix until well combined. Drop mixture by heaping tablespoonfuls onto prepared baking sheet. Let set (about 1 hour).

3. Melt the chocolate in a 1 quart oven proof saucepan using the oven method described on page 245. Dip each candy into chocolate, making sure to coat entire piece. Shake off excess, and place on prepared baking sheet to set (about 2 hours).

4. Do NOT cover the candies until the chocolate has set and dried. Store between sheets of wax paper in an airtight tin, plastic craft container with lid, cardboard box with lid, or foil covered container. Keep in a cool, dry, dark place (i.e. closed kitchen cabinet), for up to 4 weeks. Do not refrigerate or freeze.

Lander's Swiss Cream Nougats

✓
Favorite

*We like to coat these candies in dark chocolate,
but the creamy almond nougat center is delicious all by itself!*

1. Place marshmallow cream in a medium sized mixing bowl, and set aside. Line a 9 x 13 inch pan with foil, leaving a 2-inch overhang on 2 sides. Grease with butter and set aside.
To lightly toast almonds, arrange in a single layer on a foil-lined baking sheet in a 350° oven for 8-10 minutes, stirring twice. Cool completely.

2. In a heavy 2-quart saucepan, combine corn syrup and sugar. Place over high heat, and stir constantly with a wooden spoon until mixture comes to a boil. If sugar crystals are present, wipe down with a damp paper towel. Turn heat down to medium high, and cook to 275° (hard-ball stage; about 8-9 minutes), stirring occasionally. Remove from heat, and let stand undisturbed for 3 minutes. Without scraping, pour entire batch into marshmallow cream, and stir with a clean wooden spoon until smooth. Add butter, vanilla, salt and nuts, and mix until butter is incorporated. Pour into prepared pan. Allow to stand at room temperature until firm (about 4 hours).

3. Remove candy from pan using foil edges to lift. Transfer to a flat cutting surface. Remove foil and use a cleaver or heavy duty knife to cut candy into 70 pieces (10 rows by 7 rows). Melt chocolate in a 1 quart oven proof saucepan, using the oven method described on page 245. Dip each candy into chocolate, making sure to coat entire piece. Shake off excess, and place on wax or parchment paper lined baking sheet to set (about 2 hours).

4. Do NOT cover the candies until the chocolate has set and dried. Store between sheets of wax paper in an airtight tin, plastic craft container with lid, cardboard box with lid, or foil covered container. Keep in a cool, dry, dark place (i.e. closed kitchen cabinet), for up to 4 weeks. Do not refrigerate or freeze.

**3 Cups Marshmallow Cream
(About 10.5 oz.)
1 1/2 Cups Light Corn Syrup
1 1/2 Cups Sugar
1/4 Cup Melted Butter
1 Tsp. Vanilla
1/2 Tsp. Salt
1 Cup Whole Toasted Almonds
16 oz. Dark Chocolate**

tip

Perform the candy thermometer test on page 246 to determine the proper cooking temperature at your altitude.

tip

To measure corn syrup, spray the inside of the measuring cup with nonstick cooking spray, so the syrup will slide right out and not stick to the cup.

☑ Favorite

*A modern version of the popular "buckeye" candy,
teams peanut butter and chocolate for an "oh so yummy" treat!*

2/3 Cup Creamy Peanut Butter
1/4 Cup Soft Butter
1/2 Cup Coarsely Chopped Dry
    Roasted or Cocktail
    Peanuts
1 Tsp. Vanilla
2 1/4 Cups Sifted Powdered
    Sugar
16 oz. Milk Chocolate

Squiggle Topping:
1 Cup Peanut Butter Flavored
    Baking Chips
1 Tbls. Half n' Half

tip

*For test purposes, we used
Reese's Brand Peanut Butter
Flavored Baking Chips.*

1. Chop peanuts with a chef's knife on a cutting board (see page 240). Line an 8-inch square pan with foil, leaving a 2-inch overhang on 2 sides. Grease with butter and set aside.

2. In a large mixing bowl, with a heavy duty mixer, combine peanut butter, butter, peanuts and vanilla. Beat well. Add powdered sugar, 1/2 cup at a time, and beat until dough becomes stiff and crumbly. At this time, you can add more peanut butter for taste and extra creaminess.

3. Use fingers to pat mixture into prepared pan. Compress with a spatula. Cover and refrigerate 1 hour (or overnight). Remove candy from pan using foil edges to lift. Transfer to a flat cutting surface, remove foil, and use a sharp edge to cut off and discard uneven edges. Cut remaining candy into 49 pieces (7 rows by 7 rows).

4. Melt chocolate in a 1 quart oven proof saucepan using the oven method described on page 245. Dip each candy into chocolate, making sure to coat entire piece. Shake off excess, and place on wax or parchment paper lined baking sheet to set (about 2 hours). Combine peanut butter chips and half n' half in a small microwave safe measuring cup. Microwave on HIGH 60 seconds, stirring after 30 seconds. Transfer to a plastic squeeze bottle, and create squiggles on tops of candies. Let set (about 30 minutes).

5. Do NOT cover the candy until the chocolate has set and dried. Store between sheets of wax paper in an airtight tin, plastic craft container with lid, or foil covered container. Keep in the refrigerator for up to 3 weeks. Do not freeze or store at room temperature.

Drew's Peanut Butter Creams

This creamy candy sensation, tastes just like the popular chocolate covered peanut butter candy bar.

1. Place mini candy cups evenly spaced on a large baking sheet.

2. In a microwave safe medium sized bowl, combine all of the ingredients. Microwave on HIGH for 2 minutes, stirring every 30 seconds, until smooth. Let cool 3 minutes. Spoon into candy cups to 2/3 full. Chill until set (about 1 hour).

3. Do NOT cover the candy until the chocolate has set and dried. Store between sheets of wax paper in an airtight tin, plastic craft container with lid, or foil covered container. Keep in the refrigerator for up to 4 weeks. Do not freeze or store at room temperature.

10 or 12 oz. Pkg. Premier White Baking Chips
1 Cup Semi-Sweet Chocolate Chips
1 Cup Creamy Peanut Butter

44 Mini Candy Cups

This super easy penouche nugget candy is heavenly!

√
Favorite

2 Cups Heavy Whipping Cream
2 Tbls. Light Corn Syrup
2 Cups Sugar
1 Cup Packed Brown Sugar
1/4 Cup Soft Butter
4 oz. Vanilla Flavored Almond
    Bark Coating, Broken into
    1 Inch Pieces
1 1/2 Cups Toasted Pecan
    Halves

tip

Toasting the nuts enhances their flavor. To toast pecans, place nut halves in a single layer on a foil lined baking sheet in a 350° oven for 5-8 minutes, stirring occasionally, or until golden brown. Always cool completely before combining them.

tip

Perform the candy thermometer test on page 246 to determine the proper cooking temperature at your altitude.

1. Line an 8-inch square pan with foil leaving a 2 inch overhang on 2 sides. Grease with butter and set aside.

2. In a heavy 4 quart saucepan, combine cream, corn syrup and sugars. Place over medium heat, and stir with a wooden spoon until mixture comes to a boil. If sugar crystals are present, wipe down sides of pan with a wet paper towel.

3. Cook, stirring occasionally to 236° (soft-ball stage). Remove from heat. Without stirring, add butter. Let mixture stand until thermometer cools to 210° (about 1 minute). Without stirring, add almond bark coating. Let stand 1 more minute. Remove thermometer. Add nuts and stir with a wooden spoon, until the almond bark is melted and butter is mixed in. Candy will be thick and creamy. Spread into prepared pan. Refrigerate 2 hours to set.

4. Remove candy from pan using foil edges to lift. Transfer to a flat cutting surface. Remove foil and use a cleaver or heavy duty knife to cut candy into 1 inch pieces.

5. Store between sheets of wax paper in an airtight container in the refrigerator, for up to 3 weeks. To freeze, individually wrap large cut pieces (2 inches x 4 inches) in plastic food wrap, and store in an airtight container in the freezer up to 6 months. Do not store candy at room temperature.

Caution

Using a wooden spoon is essential; the handle won't get HOT during the stirring process.

*Box up these coconut filled chocolates
for a special gift!*

1. Place candy cups 1 inch apart on 10 x 15 x 1 inch jelly roll pan. To toast almonds, arrange nuts in a single layer on a foil lined baking sheet in a 350° oven for 8-10 minutes, stirring 2 or 3 times, until desired flavor is reached. Cool completely.

2. In a heavy 2-quart saucepan, combine corn syrup and marshmallows. Cook over medium heat, and stir with a wooden spoon until marshmallows are melted. Remove from heat and immediately add vanilla, almond extract and coconut. Stir until well combined. Refrigerate 30 minutes.

3. Use a small cookie scoop to shape candy into 1 inch balls. Flatten slightly and set aside. Melt the chocolate in a 1 quart oven proof saucepan using the oven method described on page 245. Dip the balls in chocolate to cover completely. Shake off excess, and place in candy cups. Press 1 almond in the top of each coated candy (see photo). Let set (about 2 hours).

4. Do NOT cover the candies until the chocolate has set and dried. Store between sheets of wax paper in an airtight tin, plastic craft container with lid, cardboard box with lid, or foil covered container. Keep in a cool, dry, dark place (i.e. closed kitchen cabinet), for up to 4 weeks. Do not refrigerate or freeze.

1/2 Cup Light Corn Syrup
12 Large Marshmallows
2 Cups Sweetened Flaked
   Coconut (About 5 oz.)
1 Tsp. Vanilla
1/2 Tsp. Almond Extract
1/2 Cup Whole Almonds,
   Toasted
12 oz. Dark or Milk Chocolate

Mini Candy Cups

tip
To measure corn syrup, spray the inside of the measuring cup with nonstick cooking spray so the syrup will slide right out and not stick to the cup.

tip
For test purposes, we used Hershey's Brand Special Dark Chocolate Bars.

Caution
Almond extract is potent; measure it carefully.

*Candied cherries team with marzipan to create
incredibly easy to make chocolates.*

12 Candied Cherries
3 Tbls. Brandy
7 oz. Marzipan
8 oz. Dark Chocolate

tip

*Marzipan is a packaged candy
dough made from sugar and
almonds. It can be found in
the baking section of your local
supermarket.*

tip

*For test purposes we used
a Hershey's Brand Special
Dark Chocolate Bar.*

Variation

*Try substituting rum
for the brandy.*

1. Line a baking sheet with parchment paper. Spray with nonstick cooking spray and set aside.

2. Cut the cherries in half, and place them in a small bowl with the brandy. Stir to coat. Set aside for 2 hours to soak, stirring occasionally.

3. Divide the marzipan into 24 equal sized pieces. Roll each into a ball, and press a marinated cherry half into the top of each ball. Melt the chocolate in a 1 quart oven proof saucepan using the oven method described on page 245.

4. Dip each cherry candy into chocolate, making sure to coat entire piece. Shake off excess, and place on prepared baking sheet to set (about 2 hours).

5. Do NOT cover the candies until the chocolate has set and dried. Store between sheets of wax paper in an airtight tin, plastic craft container with lid, cardboard box with lid, or foil covered container. Keep in a cool, dry, dark place (i.e. closed kitchen cabinet), for up to 4 weeks. Do not refrigerate or freeze.

Hartzel's Maple Nut Creams

Favorite

This candy provides a melt-in-your-mouth experience bursting with maple flavor and chocolate!

1. Line a baking sheet with wax or parchment paper. To toast walnuts, arrange whole nuts in a single layer on a foil-lined baking sheet in a 350° oven for 5-8 minutes, stirring occasionally until golden brown. Cool completely, then coarsely chop with a chef's knife on a cutting board. Set aside.

2. In a large mixing bowl, cream the butter, powdered sugar and maple flavoring. Beat until smooth and creamy (about 2 minutes), scraping sides of bowl often. Stir in walnuts. Freeze uncovered for 10 minutes, then use a small cookie scoop to shape into 1 inch balls. Place on prepared baking sheet and freeze until firm.

3. Melt chocolate and butterscotch chips together, in a 1 quart ovenproof saucepan using the oven method described on page 245. Dip frozen balls into chocolate mixture, shaking off excess, and place in mini candy cups to set (about 2 hours). When set, use remaining chocolate to create "signature" on tops of candies (see photo).

4. Do NOT cover the candies until the chocolate has set and dried. Place candies in a 9 x 13 inch baking dish, and cover loosely with foil. Store in the refrigerator for up to 1 month. Do not store at room temperature or freeze.

1 Cup Soft Butter
4 Cups Powdered Sugar
3 Tbls. Maple Flavoring
2 Cups Toasted Walnuts,
   Coarsely Chopped
16 oz. Dark Chocolate
1 Cup Butterscotch
   Flavored Chips

Mini Candy Cups

tip
For test purposes, we used Hershey's Brand Special Dark Chocolate Bars.

tip
A plastic squeeze bottle can be used to create a "signature" design on top. This identifies the type of center and gives the chocolates a professionally finished touch.

Caution
...nd butterscotch ...will become gramy if you over stir it.

Black Bear Clusters

4 Dozen Candies

✓ Favorite 🕐 Quick n' Easy

Rich, chewy and chocolatey --
these homemade candies full of coconut and macadamias are luscious!

1 1/2 Cups Sweetened Flaked
   Coconut, Lightly Toasted
16 oz. Milk Chocolate
2 Cups Coarsely Chopped
   Roasted and Salted
   Macadamia Nuts

Mini Candy Cups

tip

These candies are so delicious,
we do not recommend any
ingredient substitutions.

storage

Note container in photo;
perfect for storing chocolates. It is
actually a bin used for storing arts and
crafts, and can be purchased at your
local craft supply or discount store.

1. To toast the coconut, preheat oven to 350°. Spread the coconut in a single layer on a foil lined shallow baking pan. Bake for 8-10 minutes, stirring twice, until light golden brown. Let cool completely. Meanwhile, chop the nuts with a chef's knife on a cutting board, and set aside. Place candy cups 1 inch apart on a baking sheet.

2. Melt the chocolate in a 1 quart ovenproof saucepan using the oven method described on page 245. Immediately add the coconut and nuts, and gently stir with a rubber spatula until well mixed.

3. Use 2 ice tea spoons (not teaspoons) to make candies; one to pick up the candy mixture, and the other to push the candy from the tip of the spoon into the candy cup. Let set (about 2 hours).

4. Do NOT cover the candies until the chocolate has set and dried. Store between sheets of wax paper in an airtight tin, plastic craft container with lid, cardboard box with lid, or foil covered container. Keep in a cool, dry, dark place (i.e. closed kitchen cabinet), for up to 4 weeks. Do not refrigerate or freeze.

Caution

The coconut will become crisper
as it cools; do not over brown.

Favorite

This candy outshines the popular nut roll candy bar!

1. Line a baking sheet with wax or parchment paper and set aside. In a large bowl, combine sugar, water, marshmallow cream, vanilla and almond extract. Knead with hands to completely combine ingredients. Mixture will be very sticky and messy, before it becomes dry. Divide mixture into 8 sections. Roll each section in powdered sugar to make it easier to handle, and then shape into ropes 9 inches long and 3/4 inch in diameter. Place on prepared baking sheet, and freeze uncovered for 90 minutes.

2. Chop the nuts with a chef's knife on a cutting board, and place in a shallow bowl. Place the caramels and half n' half in a small microwave safe bowl. Microwave on HIGH 2 minutes, 15 seconds, stirring every 60 seconds. Mixture will be runny.

3. Cut frozen ropes into 1 1/2 inch pieces. Dip each frozen piece into caramel, coating all sides, and then immediately roll in nuts, to coat completely. Place on wax or parchment paper lined baking sheet and refrigerate 2 hours.

4. Store between sheets of wax paper in an airtight container at room temperature for up to 1 week, or in the refrigerator up to 3 weeks. To freeze, wrap individual pieces in plastic food wrap, and store in an airtight container for up to 6 months.

3 Cups Sifted Powdered Sugar
2 Tsp. Water
1 (7 oz.) Jar Marshmallow Cream
1 Tsp. Vanilla
1/4 Tsp. Almond Extract
1 (14 oz.) Pkg. Caramels
2 Tbls. Half n' Half or Milk
16 oz. Can Cashew Halves and Pieces, Coarsely Chopped

tip
For test purposes, we used Kraft Brand Caramels.

Variation
For a more traditional candy, substitute peanuts for the cashews.

*Creamy milk chocolate covers a crunchy
peanut butter and coconut filling.*

1/2 Cup Soft Butter
2/3 Cup Crunchy Peanut
    Butter
1 Tbls. Vanilla
2 Tbls. Milk
2 Cups Powdered Sugar
1 Cup Graham Cracker Crumbs
1 Cup Finely Chopped
    Toasted Walnuts
2/3 Cup Sweetened Flaked
    Coconut
16 oz. Milk Chocolate
Mini Candy Cups (Optional)

1. Line baking sheets with wax or parchment paper and set aside. In a large mixing bowl, cream the butter, peanut butter and vanilla, scraping sides of bowl often. Add milk and powdered sugar, and beat until smooth.

2. Stir in graham cracker crumbs, walnuts and coconut. Mix until well combined. Use a small cookie scoop to shape mixture into 1 inch balls and place on prepared baking sheets. Chill for 30 minutes. Remove from refrigerator and let sit at room temperature about 30 minutes.

3. Melt the chocolate in a 1 quart oven proof saucepan using the oven method described on page 245. Dip each candy into the melted chocolate. Shake off excess chocolate, and place on wax or parchment paper lined baking sheets to set (about 2 hours). Transfer to mini candy cups.

4. Do NOT cover the candies until the chocolate has set and dried. Store between sheets of wax paper in an airtight tin, plastic craft container with lid, cardboard box with lid, or foil covered container. Keep in a cool, dry, dark place (i.e. closed kitchen cabinet), for up to 3 weeks. Do not refrigerate or freeze.

tip

Toasting the walnuts enhances the flavor. To toast, arrange whole nuts in a single layer on a foil-lined baking sheet in a 350° oven for 8-10 minutes, stirring 2 or 3 times, until desired flavor is reached. Cool completely. To finely chop the walnuts, use a nut mill.

Variation

*Substitute peanuts
for the walnuts.*

Caution

Do not dip COLD candy pieces in warm chocolate; the humidity will cause the chocolate to separate.

tip

You can save time (and mess) by purchasing already crushed graham cracker crumbs, located in the baking section of your local supermarket.

✓
Favorite

This chocolate and coconut crunch candy is the first to disappear from a loaded party candy tray!

1. Place candy cups 1 inch apart on baking sheets. To toast almonds, arrange nuts in a single layer on a foil-lined baking sheet in a 350˚ oven for 5-8 minutes, stirring occasionally or until golden brown. Cool completely. To toast coconut, spread in a single layer on a foil lined shallow baking pan. Bake at 350˚ for 8-10 minutes, stirring twice, until light golden brown. The coconut will become crisper as it cools. Cool completely.

2. In a large mixing bowl, combine cream cheese, butter, vanilla and powdered sugar. Beat until well combined (about 1 minute). Add cookie crumbs, flaked coconut and almonds. Mix well, scraping sides of bowl often. Tightly compress mixture into a small cookie scoop, to create 1 inch balls to be placed inside candy cups.

3. Melt chocolate in a 1 quart oven proof saucepan using the oven method described on page 245. Drape a heaping teaspoon of melted chocolate over each candy piece. Top with toasted coconut. Let candy set (about 2 hours).

4. Do NOT cover the candy until the chocolate has set and dried. Store between sheets of wax paper in an airtight tin, plastic craft container with lid, or foil covered container. Keep in the refrigerator for up to 4 weeks. Do not freeze or store at room temperature.

8 oz. Soft Cream Cheese
1/4 Cup Soft Butter
2 Tsp. Vanilla
1/2 Cup Powdered Sugar
1 (18 oz.) Package Cream
    Filled Chocolate Sandwich
    Cookies, Crushed
4 Cups Sweetened Flaked
    Coconut (About 11 oz.)
2 Cups Sliced Almonds, Toasted
16 oz. Milk Chocolate
1 1/3 Cups Sweetened Flaked
    Coconut, Toasted
    (About 3 oz.)

Mini Candy Cups

tip

To crush cookies, place in a resealable plastic bag, and crush with a rolling pin. For test purposes, we used Oreo Brand Cookies.

tip

To save time measuring coconut, purchase a 14 oz. sized bag, and reserve about 1/5 for toasting.

This version of the popular pecan turtle candy,
is worth the time and effort in the kitchen!

1 Cup Soft Butter
2 Cups Packed Brown Sugar
1 Cup Light Corn Syrup
1/2 Tsp. Salt
14 oz. Can Sweetened
    Condensed Milk
2 Tsp. Vanilla
5 Cups Whole Pecans, Toasted
16 oz. Milk Chocolate

tip

Perform the candy thermometer test on page 246 to determine the proper cooking temperature at your altitude.

tip

To measure corn syrup, spray the inside of the measuring cup with nonstick cooking spray, so the syrup will slide right out and not stick to the cup.

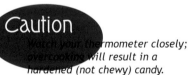

Caution

Watch your thermometer closely; overcooking will result in a hardened (not chewy) candy.

1. Line a baking sheet with parchment paper. Spray with nonstick cooking spray, and set aside. To toast pecans, place whole nuts in a single layer on a foil-lined baking sheet in a 350˚ oven for 8-10 minutes, stirring 2 or 3 times until desired flavor is reached. Cool completely. Butter the insides of a heavy 3 quart saucepan.

2. Melt the butter in the prepared saucepan over medium heat. Add brown sugar, syrup and salt and stir with a wooden spoon until sugar is dissolved. Add condensed milk and mix well. Bring mixture to a boil. Continue cooking, stirring occasionally, until thermometer reaches 238˚ (soft-ball stage; about 20 minutes). Mixture will be a dark caramel color. Immediately remove from heat and stir in vanilla and nuts until blended.

3. Working quickly, drop caramel mixture by heaping tablespoonfuls onto prepared parchment paper. Chill until firm. Remove from refrigerator and let sit 30 minutes at room temperature. Melt chocolate in a 1 quart oven proof saucepan using the oven method described on page 245. Drape 1 tablespoon chocolate on top of each candy piece. Let set (about 2 hours).

4. Do NOT cover the candies until the chocolate has set and dried. Store between sheets of wax paper in an airtight tin, plastic craft container with lid, cardboard box with lid, or foil covered container. Keep in a cool, dry, dark place (i.e. closed kitchen cabinet), for up to 4 weeks. Do not refrigerate or freeze.

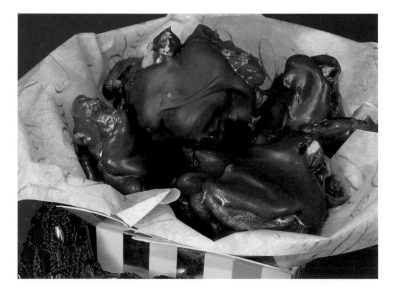

Rockypoint Candy Bites

*This impressive marshmallow filled coconut candy,
is simple to assemble, and simply irresistible!*

1. Line a 9 x 13 inch baking pan with foil, leaving a 2 inch overhang on 2 sides. Generously grease with butter. Sprinkle 1 cup coconut evenly in bottom of pan. Set aside. Use a pair of kitchen shears to cut marshmallows in half. In a 3 quart heavy saucepan, combine butter and condensed milk. Cook and stir with a wooden spoon over medium low heat, until butter is melted and mixture is smooth.

2. Remove from heat. Stir in cocoa and vanilla. Add pecans and cracker crumbs, and mix well. Quickly add marshmallows, and stir until well combined. Immediately spread mixture over coconut in prepared pan. Sprinkle remaining 1 cup coconut on top. Chill until set (about 2 hours).

3. Remove candy from pan, using foil edges to lift. Transfer to a flat cutting surface. Remove foil, and use a sharp edge to cut into 32 pieces (8 rows by 4 rows).

4. Store between sheets of wax paper in an airtight container in the refrigerator for up to 3 weeks, or in the freezer up to 2 months. Do not store at room temperature.

---

30 Large Marshmallows, Cut in Half
1/2 Cup Soft Butter
14 oz. Can Sweetened Condensed Milk
1/3 Cup Unsweetened Cocoa Powder
1 Tsp. Vanilla
1 1/4 Cups Finely Chopped Toasted Pecans
1 Cup Graham Cracker Crumbs
2 Cups Sweetened Flaked Coconut, Divided

tip

To toast pecans, place whole nuts on a foil lined baking sheet in a 350° oven for 8-10 minutes, stirring 2 or 3 times, until desired flavor is reached. Cool completely. Use a nut mill to finely chop.

Do NOT let mixture come to a boil, it will burn the cocoa.

tip

Save time, and purchase graham cracker crumbs in the baking section of your local supermarket.

These toasted nut caramel creams,
fool others into thinking you spent all day in the kitchen!

35 Caramels
1 Tbls. Soft Butter
1 1/2 Tbls. Half n' Half or Milk
1 Cup Sliced Almonds, Toasted
2/3 Cup Salted Dry Roasted
**   or Cocktail Peanuts**
2/3 Cup Roasted and Salted
**   Soy Nuts**
6 oz. Chocolate Flavored
**   Candy Coating**

Mini Candy Cups

tip

A plastic squeeze bottle can be used for squeezing melted chocolate over candies. If the chocolate becomes too thick, microwave it inside the bottle for 15 second intervals at 30% power.

1. To toast almonds, arrange nuts in a single layer on a foil-lined baking sheet in a 350° oven for 5-8 minutes, stirring occasionally or until golden brown. Cool completely.

2. In a 1 quart sized microwave size bowl, combine caramels, butter and half n' half. Microwave uncovered on HIGH for 2 minutes, stirring after 1 minute. Mixture will be boiling. Immediately stir in all nuts. Use 2 ice tea spoons (not teaspoons), one to pick up the candy mixture, and the other to push candy from the tip of the spoon into the mini candy cup.

3. Break chocolate candy coating into pieces, and place in a small sized microwave safe bowl. Microwave at 60% power for 2 1/2 minutes, stirring every 60 seconds. Immediately drizzle over candies.

4. Do NOT cover the candies until the chocolate has set and dried. Store between sheets of wax paper in an airtight container at room temperature for up to 1 week, or in the refrigerator up to 3 weeks. To freeze, wrap individual candy cups in plastic food wrap, and store in an airtight container for up to 6 months.

Variation
Substitute your favorite combination of nuts in this recipe.

Monarch's Mistletoe Candy

✓
Favorite

This layered nougat candy, features a fluffy nougat base, topped with caramel and chocolate coated pecans.

1. Line a 9-inch square pan with foil leaving a 2-inch overhang on 2 sides. Grease with butter. In a small bowl, combine powdered sugar and nonfat dry milk powder. Chop and toast pecans, and set aside.

2. In a heavy 3 quart saucepan, combine butter, sugar and corn syrup. Cook over medium high heat, and stir with a wooden spoon until sugar is dissolved and mixture comes to a boil. If there are sugar crystals present on inside of pan, wipe down with a damp paper towel. Reduce heat to medium low, and stir in powdered sugar mixture, 1 cup at a time, with vanilla, until blended. Immediately spread mixture into prepared pan. Cool (about 30 minutes). Melt chocolate in a 1 quart oven proof saucepan using the oven method described on page 245.

3. Meanwhile, place caramels in a small sized microwave safe bowl. Microwave on HIGH 1 minute 30 seconds, stirring every 30 seconds, until creamy and smooth. Evenly spread caramel mixture over cooled nougat. Let set (about 1 hour).

4. Remove chocolate from oven. Immediately stir in pecans, and then spread evenly over warm caramel layer. Let set (about 2 hours). Remove candy from pan using foil edges to lift. Transfer to a flat cutting surface. Remove foil and use a sharp edge to cut into 1 inch pieces (9 rows by 9 rows).

5. Do NOT cover the candies until the chocolate has set and dried. Store between sheets of wax paper in an airtight tin, plastic craft container with lid, cardboard box with lid, or foil covered container. Keep in a cool, dry, dark place (i.e. closed kitchen cabinet), for up to 3 weeks. Do not refrigerate or freeze.

1/2 Cup Soft Butter
1/2 Cup Sugar
1/2 Cup Light Corn Syrup
3 1/4 Cups Powdered Sugar
1/2 Cup Instant Nonfat Dry
   Milk Powder
1 Tsp. Vanilla
7 oz. Caramels (About 26)
1 Cup Coarsely Chopped
   Toasted Pecans
12 oz. Milk Chocolate

tip
Toasting the pecans enhances their flavor. First, coarsely chop nuts using a chef's knife and a cutting board. To toast, arrange chopped nuts in a single layer on a foil-lined baking sheet in a 350° oven for 5-8 minutes, stirring occasionally or until golden brown. Cool completely.

Variation
Substitute dry roasted or cocktail peanuts in place of the pecans.

tip
For test purposes, we used Kraft Brand Caramels and Hershey's Brand Milk Chocolate Bars.

✓ Favorite

*Folks look forward to these raspberry confections;
the addition of almonds makes them extra special!*

**5 Cups Sifted Powdered Sugar
4 oz. Marshmallow Cream
1 Cup Toasted Sliced
    Almonds, Broken Up
1/2 Cup Raspberry Preserves
    (With Seeds)
16 oz. Milk Chocolate**

**Mini Candy Cups (Optional)
Sprinkles**

tip
Toasting the nuts enhances their flavor. To toast almonds, place sliced nuts in a single layer on a foil-lined baking sheet in a 350˚ oven for 5-8 minutes, stirring occasionally, or until golden brown.

tip
If mixture is very soft, let balls stand for several hours to form a crust, before dipping into chocolate.

1. Line baking sheets with wax or parchment paper and set aside. In a medium sized mixing bowl, combine sugar, marshmallow cream, almonds and preserves. Stir with a wooden spoon until well combined (mixture will be stiff and sticky).

2. Use a small cookie scoop to form into 3/4 inch balls and place on prepared baking sheets. Flatten slightly with thumb. Melt chocolate in a 1 quart oven proof saucepans using the oven method described on page 245. Dip each candy piece into melted chocolate. Shake off excess, place on wax paper lined baking sheet, and immediately sprinkle with sprinkles. Let set (about 2 hours).

3. Do NOT cover the candies until the chocolate has set and dried. Store between sheets of wax paper in an airtight tin, plastic craft container with lid, cardboard box with lid, or foil covered container. Keep in a cool, dry, dark place (i.e. closed kitchen cabinet), for up to 3 weeks. Do not refrigerate or freeze.

Variation
Substitute your favorite flavor of jam in this recipe, and coat in white chocolate.

Mimi's Cherry Puff Candy

This is our favorite kid pleasing candy recipe!

1. Grease a 9 x 13" baking dish with butter and set aside.

2. In a 3-quart saucepan, combine sugar, butter, milk, 2 cups miniature marshmallows and salt. Stir with a wooden spoon over medium high heat, until mixture comes to a rapid boil.

3. Boil mixture, stirring constantly, for 5 minutes. Remove from heat. Stir in cherry chips, vanilla and 2/3 cup additional miniature marshmallows. Stir until well combined. Add more marshmallows if necessary, to thicken mixture. Pour into prepared pan. Chill until set (about 1 hour).

4. Meanwhile, in a heavy 2-quart saucepan, combine the chocolate chips and peanut butter over low heat. Stir occasionally until melted and smooth. Fold crushed peanuts into chocolate mixture. Spread evenly over cherry mixture. Let set (about 2 hours). Use a sharp edge to cut into 28 bars (7 rows by 4 rows).

5. Do NOT cover the candy until the chocolate has set and dried. Store between sheets of wax paper in an airtight tin, plastic craft container with lid, or foil covered container. Keep in the refrigerator for up to 3 weeks. Do not freeze or store at room temperature.

2 Cups Sugar
1/2 Cup Soft Butter
1 Cup Evaporated Milk
2 Cups Miniature
    Marshmallows
1/8 Tsp. Salt
1 Cup Cherry Flavored
    Baking Chips
1 Tsp. Vanilla
2/3 Cup or More Miniature
    Marshmallows
1 1/2 Cups Milk Chocolate
    Chips
3/4 Cup Creamy Peanut Butter
2 1/2 Cups Crushed Cocktail or
    Dry Roasted Peanuts

tip

To crush peanuts, place in a resealable plastic bag and roll over several times with a rolling pin for desired sized pieces.

tip

Do NOT use a heavy weight dark coated saucepan for cooking sugar mixture. It prevents the syrup from reaching the proper cooking temperature while boiling, and will result in a candy that won't set up properly.

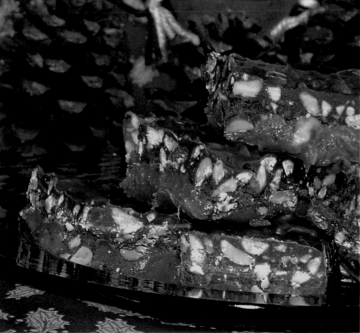

Caution
Mixture will burn if you do not stir constantly.

✓ Favorite   🕐 Quick n' Easy

This candy is so popular, it should be packaged and sold as a store bought candy bar!

16 oz. Vanilla Flavored Almond Bark Coating
2/3 Cup Creamy Peanut Butter
2 Cups Crispy Rice Cereal
1 1/2 Cups Miniature Marshmallows
1 Cup Cocktail or Dry Roasted Peanuts

8 oz. Dark or Milk Chocolate

38 Mini Candy Cups

tip

For test purposes, we used Kellogg's Brand Rice Krispies Cereal and Hershey's Brand Milk Chocolate Bars.

Variation

For a kid favorite cluster, add 1 cup candy coated miniature milk chocolate baking bits .

1. Line baking sheets with mini candy cups and set aside.

2. Break almond bark into pieces, and place in a large sized microwave safe bowl. Microwave on HIGH 2 minutes, stirring every 30 seconds, until smooth and creamy. Add peanut butter and stir until well combined. Add cereal, marshmallows and peanuts, and stir well.

3. Use 2 spoons; one to pick up the candy mixture, and the other to push candy from the tip of the spoon into the mini candy cups. Let set (about 1 hour).

4. Melt chocolate in a 1 quart oven proof saucepan, using the oven method described on page 245. Drizzle about 1 teaspoon melted chocolate on top of each candy. Let set (about 2 hours).

5. Do NOT cover the candies until the chocolate has set and dried. Store between sheets of wax paper in an airtight tin, plastic craft container with lid, cardboard box with lid, or foil covered container. Keep in a cool, dry, dark place (i.e. closed kitchen cabinet), for up to 3 weeks. Do not refrigerate or freeze.

Buffalo Crunch Candy

√ Favorite

These sweet n' salty candies have a wonderful butterscotch flavor, enhanced by, of all things, chocolate and potato sticks!

1. Line a 9 x 13 inch pan with foil, leaving a 2-inch overhang on 2 sides. Grease with butter. Combine peanuts and potato sticks in an extra large mixing bowl; set aside.

2. Combine butterscotch and white chips with peanut butter in a medium sized microwave safe mixing bowl. Microwave for 3 minutes at 70% power, stirring every 60 seconds. If necessary, microwave in 15 second increments at 70% power, until mixture is melted and smooth. Combine melted chip mixture and peanut mixture, and stir until well coated. Spread in prepared pan, and use a heavy spatula to tightly compress the mixture in the pan. Chill until set (about 1 hour). Remove from refrigerator and let sit at room temperature for 30 minutes.

3. Melt chocolate in a 1 quart oven proof saucepan using the oven method described on page 245. Remove candy from pan using foil edges to lift. Transfer to a flat cutting surface. Remove foil and use a sharp edge to cut into 90 pieces (9 rows by 10 rows). Dip the top of each candy piece into the chocolate. Place on wax paper lined baking sheets to set (about 2 hours).

4. Do NOT cover the candies until the chocolate has set and dried. Store between sheets of wax paper in an airtight tin, plastic craft container with lid, cardboard box with lid, or foil covered container. Keep in a cool, dry, dark place (i.e. closed kitchen cabinet), for up to 3 weeks. Do not refrigerate or freeze.

16 oz. Can Cocktail or Dry Roasted Peanuts
4 1/2 Cups Potato Sticks (7 oz. Can)
3 1/4 Cups Butterscotch Flavored Chips
12 oz. Pkg. Premier White Baking Chips
2/3 Cup Creamy Peanut Butter
16 oz. Milk Chocolate

tip
To measure peanut butter, pour 1/3 cup water into a 1 cup sized measuring cup. Then, add peanut butter until the water line reaches 1 cup. Drain the water and add the peanut butter to the recipe.

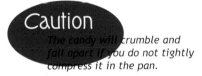

Caution
The candy will crumble and fall apart if you do not tightly compress it in the pan.

The Candy Shoppe

Here's an unforgettable cross between a fudge and a truffle!

Quick n' Easy

24 oz. Chocolate Flavored Candy Coating
1/2 Cup Evaporated Milk
1 1/2 Cups Miniature Marshmallows
1 Tsp. Vanilla

Toffee Pecan Topping:
1/3 Cup Chopped Toasted Pecans
1/3 Cup Toffee Bits

Rocky Road Topping:
1/3 Cup Coarsely Chopped Toasted Walnuts
3/4 Cup Miniature Marshmallows

tip
To toast nuts, arrange in a single layer on a foil-lined baking sheet in a 350° oven for 5-8 minutes, shaking until golden brown.

1. Line a 9-inch square pan with foil, leaving a 2-inch overhang on 2 sides. Grease with butter. In a 1 quart saucepan, combine milk and marshmallows. Heat over low heat, and stir occasionally with a wooden spoon, until marshmallows are melted.

2. Meanwhile, break chocolate candy coating into pieces and place in a medium sized microwave safe bowl. Microwave at 60% power, for 2 minutes, stirring every 60 seconds. If necessary, microwave in 15 second intervals until smooth.

3. Using a wooden spoon, stir vanilla into melted marshmallows. Pour over melted chocolate coating, and stir until well-mixed. Pour into prepared pan. Sprinkle each half of the candy mixture with separate toppings (see photo). Toppings should adhere to candy mixture. If necessary, compress with a spatula. Let set (about 2 hours).

4. Store candy inside the pan, inside a resealable plastic bag, in the refrigerator for up to 6 weeks. To serve, remove candy from pan, using foil edges to lift. Transfer to a flat cutting surface. Remove foil and use a sharp edge to cut into 81 pieces (9 rows by 9 rows). Do not store candy at room temperature or freeze.

Caution
Almond Bark coatings are all manufactured differently. If fudgits are too hard, increase milk by 2 tablespoons; if too soft, decrease milk by 2 tablespoons.

Variation
For Peppermint Topping: Sprinkle 3/4 Cup Crushed Peppermint Candies on Top.

Quick n' Easy

The possibilities for topping combinations for this creamy white candy, are endless!

1. Line a 9-inch square pan with foil, leaving a 2-inch overhang on 2 sides. Grease with butter. In a 1 quart saucepan, combine milk and marshmallows. Heat over low heat, and stir occasionally with a wooden spoon, until marshmallows are melted.

2. Meanwhile, break almond bark coating into pieces and place in medium sized microwave safe bowl. Microwave on HIGH 90 seconds. Stir well. Microwave on HIGH 60 more seconds. Stir again. If necessary, microwave in 15 second intervals until smooth.

3. Using a wooden spoon, stir vanilla into melted marshmallows. Pour over melted vanilla coating, and stir until well-mixed. Pour into prepared pan. Sprinkle each half of the candy mixture with separate toppings (see photo). Toppings should adhere to candy mixture. If necessary, compress with a spatula.

4. Store candy inside the pan, inside a resealable plastic bag, in the refrigerator for up to 6 weeks. To serve, remove candy from pan, using foil edges to lift. Transfer to a flat cutting surface. Remove foil and use a sharp edge to cut into 81 pieces (9 rows by 9 rows). Do not store candy at room temperature or freeze.

24 oz. Vanilla Flavored Almond Bark Coating
1/3 Cup Evaporated Milk
1 1/2 Cups Miniature Marshmallows
1 Tsp. Vanilla

Cherry Pecan Topping:
1/3 Cup Chopped Toasted Pecans
1/3 Cup Maraschino Cherries, Drained and Chopped

Mint Chip Topping:
3/4 Cup Creme de Menthe Baking Chips

tip

To toast nuts, arrange in a single layer on a foil-lined baking sheet in a 350° oven for 5-8 minutes, stirring until golden brown.

tip

For testing purposes, we used Andes Brand Creme de Menthe Baking Chips.

Caution
Almond Bark coatings are all manufactured differently. If fudgits are too hard, increase milk by 2 tablespoons; if too soft, decrease milk by 2 tablespoons.

This creamy white fondant recipe can be flavored into a variety of dipped chocolates.

1 Cup Heavy Whipping Cream
1/2 Cup Milk
1/3 Cup Light Corn Syrup
4 Cups Sugar
1/2 Tsp. Salt
3/4 Cup Marshmallow Cream
Various Flavorings (See Next Page)
24 oz. Milk Chocolate

tip

Perform the candy thermometer test on page 246 to determine the proper cooking temperature at your altitude.

tip

You can make 3 candies in one, by making several flavors from one batch (see next page).

1. Set aside a 9 x 13 inch ungreased glass dish. In a heavy 4-quart saucepan, combine cream, milk, corn syrup, sugar and salt. Cook over medium high heat, and stir occasionally with a wooden spoon until mixture comes to a boil. If sugar crystals are present, wipe down with a damp paper towel.

2. Cook to 238° (soft-ball stage), stirring occasionally. Immediately remove from heat, and without stirring or scraping, pour into baking dish. Set aside to cool completely (about 30-45 minutes).

3. When bottom of dish no longer feels warm, begin stirring fondant with a clean wooden spoon (you will be stirring mixture about 15-25 minutes). It may be difficult to stir at first. You don't have to stir rapidly; just keep mixture moving. After 5 minutes, add marshmallow cream and continue stirring *just until fondant mixture becomes stiff and loses most of its gloss* (it will have the appearance of a thick frosting). If flavoring the entire batch with one flavor (variations next page), you may add the flavoring shortly after the marshmallow cream is added. If you are making several flavors from one batch, see next page for instructions.

If you have stirred the fondant more than 1 hour, and it hasn't set up, you have probably under cooked the mixture. If the fondant is a bit too stiff to handle, break off small pieces and work them in your hands like modeling clay (it should soften up).

4. Form fondant into centers for chocolates (see next page). Melt chocolate in a 2 quart oven proof saucepan using the oven method described on page 245. Dip each center into chocolate, making sure to coat entire piece. Shake off excess, and place on wax or parchment paper lined baking sheet to set (about 2 hours). If desired, be sure to "sign" your chocolates (see next page).

5. Do NOT cover the candies until the chocolate has set and dried. Store between sheets of wax paper in an airtight tin, plastic craft container with lid, cardboard box with lid, or foil covered container. Keep in a cool, dry, dark place (i.e. closed kitchen cabinet), for up to 4 weeks. Do not refrigerate or freeze.

Caution

Stop stirring the fondant as soon as it loses most of its gloss. Do not wait until it has lost all of its gloss; mixture will become grainy and difficult to handle. Fondant will also continue to set up once you have stopped stirring.

Fall River Fondant Variations

The following variations are based on flavoring an entire batch one flavor. If you are dividing it into several different flavors, reduce the amounts of flavorings accordingly.

Black Walnut
1 Tbls. Vanilla
1/2 Tsp. Black Walnut Extract
1 Cup Chopped, Toasted Walnuts

Cherry Nut
1 Tbls. Almond Extract
1 Tsp. Rum Extract
1/2 Cup Chopped Candied Cherries
1 Cup Chopped, Toasted Pecans
6 Drops Red Food Coloring

Orange Cream
1 Tbls. Orange Extract
1/2 Tsp. Citric Acid
6 Drops Yellow Food Coloring
2 Drops Red Food Coloring

Making Several Flavors From One Batch

After fondant has set up, divide it into 3 balls. Press your thumb into the center of one of the portions of fondant, creating a small hole. Pour desired flavoring and color into hole along with other ingredients. Knead with your hands until well-mixed. If fondant becomes too sticky to handle, dust your hands with cornstarch or flour (powdered sugar makes the fondant stickier).

tip

Citric Acid is used for flavoring fruits, and causes fondants to become smoother. It can be found in the baking section of most health food stores, and is sometimes sold under the "Fruit Fresh" or "Produce Protection" names. Always check ingredient listings for contents.

Shaping Fondant into Centers

Cover 2 baking sheets with parchment paper and set aside. Break off about 1/2 cup of fondant. Roll into a log 1 inch thick. Use a knife to cut into 3/4 inch pieces. Roll pieces into balls in the palms of your hands. Arrange the balls on prepared baking sheets, and with your finger tips, slightly flatten each ball (see photo). This will give a more professional look to the finished chocolates. They are ready to dip into chocolate immediately, or can stand at room temperature overnight. If fondant is very soft, let stand for several hours to form a crust. At this point, fondant can be stored in the refrigerator for 3 weeks, or frozen for 6 months. Thaw at room temperature before dipping.

"Sign" Your Chocolates:
A plastic squeeze bottle can be used to create a signature design on top of the candy. This identifies the type of center, and gives the chocolates a professionally finished touch.

This creamy chocolate fondant recipe can be flavored into doubly delicious chocolate chocolates!

1 Cup Heavy Whipping Cream
1/2 Cup Milk
1/4 Cup Light Corn Syrup
3 oz. Unsweetened Baking
   Chocolate
4 Cups Sugar
1/2 Tsp. Salt
3/4 Cup Marshmallow Cream
Various Flavorings (See Next
   Page)
24 oz. Milk Chocolate

tip

Perform the candy thermometer test on page 246 to determine the proper cooking temperature at your altitude.

1. Set aside a 9 x 13 inch ungreased glass dish. In a heavy 4-quart saucepan, combine cream, milk, corn syrup, chocolate, sugar and salt. Cook over medium high heat, and stir occasionally with a wooden spoon until mixture comes to a boil. If sugar crystals are present, wipe down with a damp paper towel.

2. Cook to 236° (soft-ball stage) stirring occasionally. Immediately remove from heat, and without stirring or scraping, pour into baking dish. Set aside to cool completely (about 30-45 minutes).

3. When bottom of dish no longer feels warm, begin stirring fondant with a clean wooden spoon (you will be stirring mixture about 15-25 minutes). It may be difficult to stir at first. You don't have to stir rapidly; just keep mixture moving. After 5 minutes, add marshmallow cream and continue stirring *just until fondant mixture becomes stiff and loses most of its gloss* (it will have the appearance of a thick frosting). If flavoring the entire batch with one flavor (variations next page), you may add the flavoring shortly after the marshmallow cream is added. If you are making several flavors from one batch, see next page for instructions.

If you have stirred the fondant more than 1 hour and it hasn't set up, you have probably under cooked the mixture. If the fondant is a bit too stiff to handle, break off small pieces and work them in your hands like modeling clay (it should soften up).

4. Form fondant into centers for chocolates (see next page). Melt chocolate in a 2 quart oven proof saucepan using the oven method described on page 245. Dip each center into chocolate, making sure to coat entire piece. Shake off excess and place on wax or parchment paper lined baking sheet to set (about 2 hours). If desired, be sure to "sign" your chocolates (see next page).

5. Do NOT cover the candies until the chocolate has set and dried. Store between sheets of wax paper in an airtight tin, plastic craft container with lid, cardboard box with lid, or foil covered container. Keep in a cool, dry, dark place (i.e. closed kitchen cabinet), for up to 4 weeks. Do not refrigerate or freeze.

tip

You can make 3 candies in one, by making several flavors from one batch (see next page).

Caution

STOP stirring the fondant as soon as it loses most of its gloss. Do not wait until it has lost all of its gloss; mixture will become grainy and difficult to handle. Fondant will also continue to set up once you have stopped stirring.

Bennett's Fondant Variations

The following variations are based on flavoring an entire batch one flavor. If you are dividing it into several different flavors, reduce the amounts of flavorings accordingly.

Chocolate Nut
1 Tbls. Vanilla
1 Cup Chopped, Toasted Pecans

Chocolate Mint
2 Tsp. Pure Peppermint Extract
(NOT Mint Extract)

Rocky Road
1 Tbls. Vanilla
1 Cup Miniature Marshmallows
1 Cup Chopped, Toasted Walnuts

Making Several Flavors From One Batch

After fondant has set up, divide it into 3 balls. Press your thumb into the center of one of the portions of fondant, creating a small hole. Pour desired flavoring and color into hole along with other ingredients. Knead with your hands until well-mixed. If fondant becomes too sticky to handle, dust your hands with cornstarch or flour (powdered sugar makes the fondant stickier).

Shaping Fondant into Centers

Cover 2 baking sheets with parchment paper and set aside. Break off about 1/2 cup of fondant. Roll into a log 1 inch thick. Use a knife to cut into 3/4 inch pieces. Roll pieces into balls in the palms of your hands. Arrange the balls on prepared baking sheets, and with your finger tips, slightly flatten each ball (see photo). This will give a more professional look to the finished chocolates. They are ready to dip into chocolate immediately, or can stand at room temperature overnight. If fondant is very soft, let stand for several hours to form a crust. At this point, fondant can be stored in the refrigerator for 3 weeks, or frozen for 6 months. Thaw at room temperature before dipping.

"Sign" Your Chocolates:
A plastic squeeze bottle can be used to create a signature design on top of the candy. This identifies the type of center, and gives the chocolates a professionally finished touch.

A wonderfully buttery candy,
handed down three generations!

2 Cups Sugar
2/3 Cup Water
1/4 Tsp. Cream of Tartar
3 Tbls. Soft Butter
1 Tsp. Vanilla
1 Tsp. Maple or Butterscotch
Flavoring (Optional)

tip

Use a wooden spoon to stir this recipe, and cook over medium heat to reach desired temperature. Otherwise, mixture will burn.

tip

Perform the candy thermometer test on page 246 to determine the proper cooking temperature at your altitude.

1. Line a 9 x 13" pan with parchment paper. Grease the paper with butter, and set aside.

2. In a heavy 2 quart saucepan, combine the sugar, water and cream of tartar. Stir with a wooden spoon until sugar is dissolved. Bring to a boil without stirring, over medium high heat. Reduce heat to medium, and continue cooking until a candy thermometer reads 300° (hard crack stage). Watch the thermometer closely; the candy will begin to turn a golden color, and if you cook even slightly above 300°, the mixture will burn.

3. Immediately remove from heat, and add butter, vanilla and flavorings (optional). Stir until well mixed. Return to heat. Cook and stir constantly until thermometer returns to 300°. Pour into prepared pan.

4. Let mixture cool 6 minutes. Hold sides of paper, and remove mixture to a flat cutting surface. Use a sharp edge, to double into 60 pieces (10 rows by 6 rows). Be sure score is deep enough, so when candy has cooled completely, it will break into even pieces. Cool and break into pieces.

5. Store between sheets of wax paper in an airtight tin, plastic craft container with lid, or glass container with glass lid, at room temperature for up to 4 weeks. Do not refrigerate or freeze.

Quick n' Easy   Favorite

*The wonderful aroma of cinnamon will fill your home,
as you cook up this "red rocks" candy.*

1. Grease a 10 x 15 x 1 inch jelly roll pan with butter and set aside. Combine sugar, corn syrup and water in a 2 quart heavy saucepan. Cook over medium high heat, stirring constantly with a wooden spoon, until sugar is dissolved and mixture comes to a boil. If sugar crystals are present on inside of pan, wipe down with a damp paper towel.

2. Cook, stirring often, until mixture reaches 234° (soft-ball stage; about 10 minutes). Immediately add 1/2 cup cinnamon candies and food coloring. Cook, stirring constantly, to 300° (hard-crack stage; about 12 minutes). Remove from heat, and stir in butter until melted and combined. Quickly pour hot mixture onto prepared pan and spread thin. Immediately sprinkle with remaining cinnamon candies. Let cool completely (about 1 hour).

3. When completely cooled, break into bite-sized pieces. Wrap in colored cellophane with ribbon ties.

4. Store between sheets of wax paper in an airtight tin, plastic craft container with lid, or glass container with glass lid, at room temperature for up to 4 weeks. Do not refrigerate or freeze.

2 Cups Sugar
1 Cup Light Corn Syrup
1/2 Cup Water
1 Cup Red Cinnamon Candies,
    Divided (9 oz. Bag)
5 Drops Red Food Coloring
1 Tbls. Soft Butter

Colored Cellophane and
    Ribbon Ties (Optional)

tip

For test purposes, we used Brach's Brand Cinnamon Imperials.

tip

To measure corn syrup, spray the inside of the measuring cup with nonstick cooking spray, so the syrup will slide right out, and not stick to the cup.

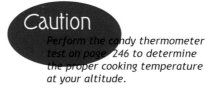

Caution

Perform the candy thermometer test on page 246 to determine the proper cooking temperature at your altitude.

Someone Deserves a Break Today...

Offer to baby sit for a friend or neighbor.
Cook up the super easy "Rocky Ford Fudge" on Page 53,
or "Twin Peaks Truffles" on Page 66.
Children of all ages will have fun,
and a friend will get a much needed break!

Fudges and Truffles

Prepare for the "oohs" and the "aahs".
Without a doubt, more fudge is made in homes than
any other holiday candy.
The most elegant candies you can make are truffles.
Our recipes are easy and require little experience.

✓
Favorite

Rich - - Creamy - - and Dreamy - -
describe this fabulous triple chocolate fudge!

1/3 Cup Soft Butter
2 1/4 Cups Sugar
1 Cup Evaporated Milk
1/2 Tsp. Salt
7 oz. Marshmallow Cream
8 oz. German Sweet
   Chocolate, Chopped
3 (1.45 oz.) Chocolate Candy
   Bars with Almonds,
   Chopped
1 Cup Semisweet Chocolate
   Chips
2 Cups Toasted Almonds,
   Chopped
2 Tsp. Vanilla

tip

We recommend using a Timer with this recipe (see page 241). Use a chef's knife and cutting board to chop chocolate, candy bars and almonds (see page 240).

Caution

Wait for mixture to reach a rapid boil before timing 5 minutes. Otherwise fudge may not set up properly.

1. Line a 9 x 13 inch pan with foil, leaving a 2 inch overhang on 2 sides. Grease with butter and set aside. Toasting the almonds enhances their flavor. To toast, arrange whole nuts in a single layer on a foil-lined baking sheet in a 350° oven for 8-10 minutes, stirring 2 or 3 times, until desired flavor is reached. Always cool completely before adding to the recipe.

2. In a heavy 3 quart saucepan, combine butter, sugar, milk and salt. Cook over medium heat, and stir constantly with a wooden spoon until sugar is dissolved. If sugar crystals are present on side of pan, wipe down with a damp paper towel. Bring to a rapid boil, and boil for 5 minutes, stirring constantly. See Caution Below. Remove from heat (mixture is very hot).

3. Add and gently stir in order, marshmallow cream, chocolate, candy bars and chips until chocolate is melted and mixture is blended (do NOT over stir as mixture can become grainy). Fold in almonds and vanilla. Immediately spread into prepared pan. Cool completely (about 1 hour). Remove fudge from pan, using foil edges to lift. Transfer to a flat cutting surface. Remove foil and use a sharp edge to cut into 1 inch squares.

4. Store between sheets of wax paper in an airtight container at room temperature for up to 1 week, or in the refrigerator up to 3 weeks. To freeze, wrap larger cut pieces in plastic wrap and store in an airtight container for up to 6 months.

Variation

Add 2/3 cup chopped candied cherries for a cherry chocolate fudge.

tip

For test purposes, we used Baker's Brand German Sweet Baking Chocolate, and Hershey's Brand Chocolate Candy Bars with Almonds.

Rocky Ford Fudge

Quick n' Easy   Favorite

This no-fail old-fashioned fudge is totally irresistible!

1. Line a 9-inch square pan with foil, leaving a 2 inch overhang on 2 sides. Grease with butter and set aside.

2. In a heavy 2 quart saucepan, combine condensed milk, chocolate pieces and salt. Place over low heat, and stir occasionally with a wooden spoon until chocolate is melted.

3. Remove from heat and gently stir until smooth. Stir in vanilla and nuts. Pour into prepared pan. Refrigerate 2 hours, until firm.

4. Remove fudge from pan using foil edges to lift. Transfer to a flat cutting surface. Remove foil and use a sharp edge to cut into 1 inch squares.

5. Store between sheets of wax paper in an airtight container at room temperature for up to 3 days, or in the refrigerator up to 3 weeks. To freeze, wrap cut pieces in plastic wrap, and store in an airtight container for up to 6 months.

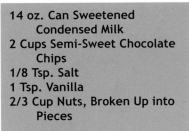

14 oz. Can Sweetened
    Condensed Milk
2 Cups Semi-Sweet Chocolate
    Chips
1/8 Tsp. Salt
1 Tsp. Vanilla
2/3 Cup Nuts, Broken Up into
    Pieces

tip

For less mess, use a small wax paper square dipped in soft butter to grease the foil lining in the pan.

Nothing compares to this German Chocolate fudge,
complete with coconut and pecans.

✓ Favorite

2 1/4 Cups Sugar
3/4 Cup Evaporated Milk
2 Tbls. Soft Butter
1/4 Tsp. Salt
1 Cup Semisweet Chocolate
    Chips
6 oz. German Sweet Baking
    Chocolate, Chopped
4 oz. Marshmallow Cream
1 Cup Coarsely Chopped
    Toasted Pecans
1 Cup Toasted Sweetened
    Flaked Coconut

tip
For test purposes, we used Baker's Brand German Sweet Baking Chocolate.

tip
We recommend using a Timer with this recipe (see page 241). Use a chef's knife and cutting board to chop pecans and chocolate (see page 240).

Caution
Wait for mixture to reach a rapid boil before timing 6 minutes. Otherwise, fudge may not set up properly. Do not over cook, as mixture will turn crumbly.

1. Line a 9-inch square pan with foil, leaving a 2 inch overhang on 2 sides. Grease with butter and set aside. Toasting the pecans and coconut enhances their flavor. To toast, arrange whole nuts and coconut (in separate sections) in a single layer on a foil-lined baking sheet in a 350° oven for 8-10 minutes, stirring 2 or 3 times, until desired flavor is reached. Always cool completely before adding to the recipe.

2. In a heavy 2 quart saucepan, combine sugar, milk, butter and salt. Cook over medium heat, and stir constantly with a wooden spoon, until sugar is dissolved. If sugar crystals are present on inside of pan, wipe down with a damp paper towel. Bring to a rapid boil, reduce heat to medium low, and boil for 6 minutes (see Caution below), stirring occasionally. Remove from heat.

3. Combine chips, baking chocolate, marshmallow cream, and pecans in a large mixing bowl. Pour hot sugar mixture over chocolate mixture. Beat with a wooden spoon, until it thickens and begins to lose its gloss (about 2 minutes). Immediately spread into prepared pan, and sprinkle with toasted coconut. Compress with a spatula. Cool completely (about 1 hour).

4. Remove fudge from pan using foil edges to lift. Transfer to a flat cutting surface. Remove foil and use a sharp edge to cut into 1 inch squares.

5. Store between sheets of wax paper in an airtight container at room temperature for up to 1 week, or in the refrigerator up to 3 weeks. To freeze, wrap larger cut pieces in plastic wrap and store in an airtight container for up to 6 months.

*A rich chocolate butterscotch confection with a
candy bar in the middle - - you'll love this fudge!*

1. Line an 8-inch square pan with foil, leaving a 2 inch overhang on 2 sides. Grease with butter and set aside. Chop peanuts and candy bars, and set aside.

2. In a heavy 3 quart saucepan, combine sugar, milk, butter and salt. Cook over medium heat, and stir constantly with a wooden spoon, until sugar is dissolved. If sugar crystals are present on side of pan, wipe down with a damp paper towel. Bring mixture to a rapid boil, and boil for 5 minutes (see Caution below), stirring occasionally. Remove from heat.

3. Gently stir in marshmallow cream. Add chocolate chips, butterscotch chips, peanuts and vanilla. Gently stir until chips are melted, and mixture is blended (do NOT over stir as mixture can become grainy). Immediately pour half the mixture into prepared pan. Quickly sprinkle chopped candy bars evenly over mixture. Spread remaining half of fudge over candy bars. Refrigerate until firm (about 2 hours).

4. Remove fudge from pan using foil edges to lift. Transfer to a flat cutting surface. Remove foil and use a sharp edge to cut into 1 inch squares. Wrap in foil squares (see photo).

5. Store between sheets of wax paper in an airtight container at room temperature for up to 1 week, or in the refrigerator up to 3 weeks. To freeze, wrap larger cut pieces in plastic wrap and store in an airtight container for up to 6 months.

1 1/2 Cups Sugar
2/3 Cup Evaporated Milk
3 Tbls. Soft Butter
1/2 Tsp. Salt
7 oz. Marshmallow Cream
3/4 Cup Semisweet Chocolate
    Chips
3/4 Cup Butterscotch Flavored
    Chips
2/3 Cup Chopped Cocktail or
    Dry Roasted Peanuts
1 Tsp. Vanilla
3 (2.05 oz.) Chocolate
    Covered Peanut Nougat
    Candy Bars, Chopped
Colored Foil Squares

tip
For test purposes, we used Snickers Brand Candy Bars.

tip
We recommend using a Timer with this recipe (see page 241). Use a chef's knife and cutting board to chop peanuts and candy bars (see page 240).

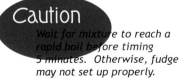
Caution
Wait for mixture to reach a rapid boil before timing 5 minutes. Otherwise, fudge may not set up properly.

*Although macadamia nuts are expensive,
they are worth it, in this fudge laced with a touch of honey.*

1/3 Cup Half n' Half
1/3 Cup Milk
1 1/2 Cups Sugar
1 Cup Packed Brown Sugar
3 Tbls. Honey
2 Tbls. Soft Butter
1 Tsp. Vanilla
1 Cup Coarsely Chopped
    Roasted and Salted
    Macadamia Nuts, Divided

tip

When cooking candy, always place the liquids in the pan first, then the sugar. This will eliminate sugar crystals from forming on the sides of the cooking pan.

tip

Perform the candy thermometer test on page 246 to determine the proper cooking temperature at your altitude.

1. Chop nuts with a chef's knife on a cutting board. Line a 9 x 5 x 3 inch loaf pan with foil, leaving a 2-inch overhang on 2 sides. Grease with butter and set aside.

2. Butter the insides of a heavy 2-quart saucepan. In the saucepan, combine half n' half, milk, sugar, brown sugar and honey. Cook and stir with a wooden spoon over medium high heat, until mixture boils and sugars dissolve. Reduce heat to medium-low. Continue to boil at a steady rate, stirring frequently, until thermometer reaches 236° (soft-ball stage; about 20 minutes).

3. Remove pan from heat (mixture is very hot). Carefully add the butter and vanilla, but do not stir. Cool, without stirring, to 120° (about 45 minutes). Remove thermometer from pan. Beat mixture vigorously with a clean wooden spoon, until fudge begins to thicken (it will be very stiff at first). Add 1/2 cup nuts. Continue beating until fudge starts to lose its gloss (about 8 minutes). Immediately spread fudge evenly in prepared pan. Sprinkle with remaining nuts. Let set (about 1 hour). When fudge is firm, remove from pan using foil edges to lift. Transfer to a flat cutting surface. Remove foil and use a cleaver or heavy duty knife to cut fudge into 36 pieces (9 rows by 4 rows).

4. Store between sheets of wax paper in an airtight container at room temperature for up to 3 days, or in the refrigerator up to 3 weeks. To freeze, wrap cut pieces in plastic wrap and store in an airtight container for up to 6 months.

Favorite

One bite, and you'll be hooked on this
10 minute fluffy white fudge!

1. Line an 8-inch square pan with foil, leaving a 2 inch overhang on 2 sides. Grease with butter and set aside. Toasting the pecans or walnuts enhances their flavor. To toast, arrange whole nuts in a single layer on a foil-lined baking sheet in a 350° oven for 8-10 minutes, stirring 2 or 3 times, until desired flavor is reached. Always cool completely before adding to the recipe. Use a chef's knife and cutting board to coarsely chop.

2. In a large mixing bowl, beat cream cheese until fluffy (about 1 minute); set aside. Break almond bark into pieces, and place in a medium sized microwave safe bowl. Microwave on HIGH 90 seconds. Stir well. Microwave on HIGH 60 more seconds. Stir again. If necessary, microwave in 15 second intervals until smooth and creamy. Add butter, and gently stir until butter is melted.

3. Immediately pour almond bark mixture over cream cheese. Beat until smooth, and mixture begins to set up (about 4-5 minutes). Stir in nuts. Immediately spread evenly into prepared pan. Cool at room temperature about 30 minutes. Refrigerate until set (about 2 hours).

4. Remove fudge from pan using foil edges to lift. Transfer to a flat cutting surface. Remove foil and use a sharp edge to cut into 1 inch squares (8 rows by 8 rows).

5. Store between sheets of wax paper in an airtight container in the refrigerator up to 4 weeks. Do not freeze or store at room temperature.

8 oz. Soft Cream Cheese
    (Do NOT Use Low Fat)
34 oz. Vanilla Flavored Almond
    Bark Coating
3 Tbls. Soft Butter
1 1/2 Cups Coarsely Chopped
    Pecans or Walnuts,
    Toasted

tip
Can microwave butter separately at 40% power for 20 seconds, to assure it melts quickly into the almond bark mixture.

Caution
Do not use low fat cream cheese; it will affect the taste and texture.

64 Fudge Pieces

☑
Favorite

This creamy peanut butter fudge can also be rolled into balls and coated in milk chocolate.

1 1/4 Cups Milk
1/3 Cup Light Corn Syrup
1/4 Cup Soft Butter
Pinch of Baking Soda
3 Cups Sugar
1 Cup Packed Brown Sugar
1 Cup Creamy Peanut Butter
1 Tsp. Vanilla
1 Cup Coarsely Chopped Dry
    Roasted or Cocktail
    Peanuts

tip

When cooking candy, always place the liquids in the pan first, then the sugar. This will minimize sugar crystals from forming on the inside of the cooking pan.

tip

To coarsely chop peanuts, place in a resealable plastic bag and roll over several times with a rolling pin for desired sized pieces (see page 240).

1. Set aside a 9 x 13 inch ungreased baking pan. Line an 8-inch square pan with foil, leaving a 2-inch overhang on 2 sides. Grease with butter and set aside. Butter insides of a heavy 4 quart saucepan.

2. In saucepan combine milk, corn syrup, butter, baking soda and sugars. Place over medium-high heat, and stir occasionally with a wooden spoon, until mixture comes to a boil. If sugar crystals are present, wipe down with a damp paper towel.

3. Turn heat down to medium, and cook, stirring constantly, until temperature reaches 234° (soft-ball stage; about 11-12 minutes). Immediately pour mixture without scraping sides of pan, into a 9 x 13 inch baking pan. Cool until bottom of pan feels warm, but not hot (about 20 minutes).

4. Using a wooden spoon and working quickly, stir in peanut butter, vanilla and nuts. Continue stirring just until mixture is smooth (do NOT wait until it loses it's gloss). Over stirring will result in a hardened candy.

5. Pour into foil lined pan and let cool. Refrigerate until firm. Remove fudge from pan using foil edges to lift. Transfer to a flat cutting surface. Remove foil and use a sharp edge to cut into 1 inch pieces (8 rows by 8 rows).

6. Store cut pieces between sheets of wax paper in an airtight container at room temperature for up to 1 week, or in the refrigerator up to 3 weeks. To freeze, wrap cut pieces in plastic wrap and store in an airtight container for up to 6 months.

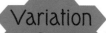

Variation

Once mixture has been stirred, it can be formed into balls. Let sit 1 hour until hardened, then dip in melted chocolate.

Favorite

Try this chocolate fudge with a creamy peanut butter layer in the middle.

1. Line a 9-inch square pan with foil, leaving a 2 inch overhang on 2 sides. Grease with butter and set aside.

2. In a heavy 3 quart saucepan, combine sugar, milk and butter. Cook over medium heat, and stir constantly with a wooden spoon until sugar is dissolved. If sugar crystals are present on inside of pan, wipe down with a damp paper towel. Bring to a rapid boil, turn heat down to medium low, and boil for 6 minutes, stirring occasionally. While mixture is boiling, combine peanut butter and powdered sugar in 2 cup sized (see tip below) microwave safe measuring cup. Stir until well combined. Microwave at 50% power for 40 seconds, then stir. Microwave at 50% power for 1 minute more, then stir and set aside.

3. Remove sugar mixture from heat. Stir in marshmallow cream, and vanilla. Add chips, and gently stir until chocolate is melted, and mixture is blended (do NOT over stir as mixture can become grainy). Immediately pour half of the chocolate mixture into prepared pan. Dollop warm peanut butter mixture on top. Spread remaining chocolate mixture over peanut butter. Use a toothpick to swirl entire mixture, so peanut butter mixture swirls into chocolate (see photo). Chill until firm (about 2 hours).

4. Remove fudge from pan using foil edges to lift. Transfer to a flat cutting surface. Remove foil and use a sharp edge to cut into 1 1/4 inch squares.

5. Store between sheets of wax paper in an airtight container in the refrigerator up to 3 weeks. For best results, do not freeze, or store at room temperature.

2 Cups Sugar
3/4 Cup Evaporated Milk
1/2 Cup Soft Butter
6 oz. Marshmallow Cream
2 Tsp. Vanilla
1 1/2 Cups Semisweet
 Chocolate Chips

3/4 Cup Creamy Peanut
 Butter
1/3 Cup Powdered Sugar

tip

To measure peanut butter, pour 1/2 cup water in a 2 cup sized measuring cup. Then, add peanut butter until the water line reaches the 1 1/4 cup line. Drain the water and add the powdered sugar to the cup.

Variation

To enhance the peanut flavor, add 1/2 cup chopped cocktail or dry roasted peanuts to the chocolate fudge.

Caution

Add the marshmallow cream first to the hot mixture; otherwise you risk burning the chocolate.

☑
Favorite

This delectable 2 layered chocolate fudge is easy to make, and features a marshmallow candy topping.

Bottom Layer:
1/2 Cup Evaporated Milk
1/4 Cup Soft Butter
1 1/2 Cups Sugar
22 Large Marshmallows, Cut in Half
1 Cup Semisweet Chocolate Chips
1 Tsp. Vanilla

Top Layer:
12 oz. Milk Chocolate
1 1/4 Cups Miniature Marshmallows
1/2 Cup Red and Green Candy Coated Milk Chocolate Pieces

Mini Candy Cups (Optional)

tip

For test purposes, we used Hershey's Brand Milk Chocolate Bars and M&M's Brand Candy Pieces.

tip

When cooking candy, always place the liquids in the pan first, then the sugar. This will minimize sugar crystals from forming on the inside of the cooking pan.

Variation

For mint fudge, add 1 tsp. pure peppermint extract in place of the vanilla, and 3/4 Cup Crushed Peppermint Candies in place of the miniature marshmallows.

Caution

We recommend using a Timer with this recipe (see page 241). Wait for mixture to reach a rapid boil before timing 5 minutes. Otherwise, fudge may not set up properly.

1. Line an 8-inch square pan with foil, leaving a 2 inch overhang on 2 sides. Grease with butter and set aside. Use kitchen shears to cut the large marshmallows in half; set aside.

2. Melt the milk chocolate in a 2 quart oven proof saucepan using the oven method described on page 245. Meanwhile, in a 2 quart heavy saucepan, combine milk, butter and sugar. Cook over medium high heat, and stir constantly with a wooden spoon, until mixture comes to a boil. Boil for 5 minutes. Remove from heat.

3. Use a clean wooden spoon to add and combine in order, cut marshmallows, chocolate chips and vanilla. Gently stir until melted and smooth. Pour into prepared pan.

4. Immediately remove melted chocolate from oven, and stir in miniature marshmallows. Spread evenly over fudge mixture in pan. Sprinkle with candies. Use a spatula to press candies into warm chocolate. Let set (about 2 hours).

5. Remove candy from pan using foil edges to lift. Transfer to a flat cutting surface. Remove foil and use a sharp edge to cut into 1 inch pieces (8 rows by 8 rows). Place in mini candy cups.

6. Store between sheets of wax paper in an airtight container in the refrigerator up to 4 weeks. Do not store at room temperature or freeze.

Evergreen Ice Cream Fudge

✓ Favorite

This fudge doubles as an elegant dessert. Feel free to experiment with combinations of different kinds of chocolate and ice cream flavors.

1. Chop all nuts and set aside. Arrange candy cups in rows on a large baking sheet. Melt chocolate in a 2 quart ovenproof saucepan using the oven method described on page 245. Remove from oven and add ice cream, but do NOT stir. Let sit 5-7 minutes, or until ice cream is visibly semi-melted.

2. Gently stir the mixture with a rubber spatula, until smooth. Fold in coarsely chopped nuts. Refrigerate until mixture is cool (about 30 minutes).

3. Using a small cookie scoop, drop cold mixture by rounded scoopfuls into candy cups. Sprinkle with nuts. Place candies in freezer until frozen (about 2 hours).

4. Store between sheets of wax paper in an airtight container in the freezer for up to 4 months. Let candies sit at room temperature for 10 minutes before serving. Do not store at room temperature or in the refrigerator.

24 oz. Milk Chocolate
1 Cup Soft Vanilla Ice Cream
    Brand Name Only
3/4 Cup Coarsely Chopped
    Walnuts
3/4 Cup Finely Chopped
    Walnuts
60 Candy Cups

tip

To coarsely chop nuts, place in a resealable plastic bag and roll over several times with a rolling pin for desired sized pieces. To finely chop nuts, use a nut mill (see page 240).

Variation
Try white chocolate with mint chocolate chip ice cream - - it is one of our favorites!

Quick n' Easy

A fabulous cherry nut fudge that is created in less than 15 minutes!

14 oz. Can Sweetened
   Condensed Milk
3 Cups Semisweet Chocolate
   Chips
2 1/2 Cups Miniature
   Marshmallows or 18 Large
   Marshmallows, Cut in Half
1 Tsp. Vanilla
1 Cup Whole Pistachio Nuts
   (About 8 oz. Nuts in Shell)
1/2 Cup Chopped Candied
   Cherries

tip

For less mess, use a small waxed paper square to spread the soft butter on the foil lining in the pan.

1. Line a 9-inch square pan with foil, leaving a 2 inch overhang on 2 sides. Grease with butter and set aside.

2. Place sweetened condensed milk, chocolate chips and marshmallows in a medium sized microwave safe mixing bowl. Stir ingredients together to combine. Microwave uncovered on HIGH for 1 minute. Stir well. Microwave on HIGH for 2 more minutes, stirring every minute, until melted and smooth.

3. Gently stir in vanilla, nuts and cherries. Immediately pour mixture into prepared pan. Use a knife to spread mixture evenly to all edges of the pan. Let set (about 1 hour). Cover pan with plastic wrap, and refrigerate 2 hours, or until firm. Remove fudge from pan, using foil edges to lift. Transfer to a flat cutting surface. Remove foil and use a sharp edge to cut into 1 inch pieces.

4. Store between sheets of wax paper in an airtight container at room temperature for up to 3 days, or in the refrigerator up to 3 weeks. To freeze, wrap cut pieces in plastic wrap and store in an airtight container for up to 6 months.

Variation

Try substituting hazelnuts for the pistachios.

Byers Cream Cheese Truffles

These chocolate candies make sensational gifts.
Everyone will want to know the "secret" ingredient!

1. Line a baking sheet with mini candy cups. Finely chop the walnuts in a nut mill, and place in a shallow bowl. Put crushed peppermint candies in another shallow bowl and set aside.

2. In a large mixing bowl, beat cream cheese and vanilla. Gradually add powdered sugar and beat well, scraping sides of bowl often. Place chocolate chips in a 1 quart oven proof saucepan and melt the chocolate using the oven method described on page 245.

3. Add the melted chocolate to the cream cheese mixture, and stir with a large spoon until well combined. Cover with plastic wrap, and refrigerate for no longer than 15 minutes. Remove mixture from refrigerator, and use a small cookie scoop to shape mixture into 1 inch balls. Immediately roll in crushed peppermint or crushed nuts, and place in candy cups.

4. Store between sheets of wax paper in an airtight container in the refrigerator for up to 4 weeks. Do not freeze or store at room temperature.

8 oz. Soft Cream Cheese
1 1/2 Tsp. Vanilla
3 Cups Sifted Powdered Sugar
2 Cups Semisweet Chocolate
    Chips
1 Cup Finely Chopped Walnuts
3/4 Cup Crushed Peppermint
    Candies
48 Mini Candy Cups

tip
For testing purposes, we used Wilton Brand Peppermint Crunch Sprinkles.

tip
The sprinkles and nuts will adhere to the balls better if you hold the 1 inch balls in your closed hand for 5-10 seconds before rolling in the coatings. The heat from your hand will warm the ball just enough to make it slightly sticky.

Variation
Truffles can also be coated with flaked coconut or toffee bits.

✓ Favorite 🕐 Quick n' Easy

*Our most basic truffle recipe --
the perfect combination of chocolate and nuts!*

2/3 Cup Evaporated Milk
1/4 Cup Sugar
1 3/4 Cups Milk Chocolate
   Chips
1 Tsp. Vanilla
1 1/4 Cups Sliced Almonds,
   Toasted

26 Mini Candy Cups

Variation

*For a fancier truffle, substitute
1 tsp. almond extract for
the vanilla.*

Caution

*Mixture will burn if you boil
at a higher temperature than
medium low.*

1. Line a baking sheet with mini candy cups and set aside. Toasting the nuts enhances their flavor. To toast, arrange sliced nuts in a single layer on a foil-lined baking sheet in a 350˚ oven for 5-8 minutes, stirring occasionally, or until golden brown. Cool completely before adding to chocolate mixture.

2. Combine milk and sugar in a 1 quart heavy saucepan. Bring to a rapid boil over medium heat, stirring constantly with a wooden spoon. If sugar crystals are present on inside of pan, wipe down with a damp paper towel. Once mixture begins to boil, turn heat down to medium low, and boil for 3 minutes, stirring occasionally. Remove from heat (mixture will be hot).

3. Immediately stir in chips. Stir vigorously until mixture is smooth. Add vanilla and nuts, and stir just until well combined. Use 2 spoons, one to pick up the truffle mixture, and the other to push it from the tip of the spoon into the candy cup. Refrigerate until ready to serve.

4. Store between sheets of wax paper in a closed container in the refrigerator for up to 3 weeks. Do not freeze or store at room temperature.

*If you prefer white chocolate,
these truffles will delight you!*

1. Line a baking sheet with wax paper, and set aside. Melt the white chocolate in a 1 quart oven proof saucepan, using the oven method described on page 245. Meanwhile, heat the cream in a heavy 1 quart saucepan over low heat, until it begins to steam; do NOT allow it to boil. Remove from heat, and let sit until slightly cooled, but still very warm.

2. Immediately pour melted white chocolate into a medium sized mixing bowl. Pour warm cream over white chocolate, and beat with an electric mixer until well-blended (about 30 seconds). Add vanilla and stir well. Cool mixture in bowl, in the refrigerator about 20 minutes, or just long enough to be firm enough to handle.

3. Use a small cookie scoop to shape mixture into 1 inch balls. Place close together on prepared baking sheet. Refrigerate 2 hours, until firm. Remove from refrigerator, and let sit at room temperature for 30 minutes.

4. Melt the milk chocolate in a 1 quart oven proof saucepan, using the oven method described on page 245. Dip each truffle into milk chocolate, shaking off excess. Sprinkle with holiday sprinkles. Let set (about 2 hours). Transfer to mini candy cups.

5. Store between sheets of wax paper in a closed container in the refrigerator for up to 3 weeks. Do not freeze or store at room temperature.

16 oz. White Chocolate
1/3 Cup Whipping Cream
1 Tsp. Vanilla
8 oz. Milk Chocolate
Holiday Sprinkles

Mini Candy Cups

Variation
Depending upon your preference, substitute mint, orange, cherry or rum extract for the vanilla.

Caution
Cool mixture just long enough to handle with a small cookie scoop; over cooling will cause it to harden and set up, making it impossible to shape into truffle balls.

Raspberry lovers beware:
these truffles taste just like berries n' cream!

✓
Favorite

12 oz. White Chocolate
1/4 Cup Whipping Cream
1/4 Tsp. Citric Acid
1/2 Cup Raspberry Jam

Mini Candy Cups (Optional)

tip

For test purposes, we used Ghiradelli Brand White Chocolate Bars, and Smuckers Brand Raspberry Jam with Seeds.

tip

Citric Acid is used for flavoring fruits, and will make truffles smoother. It can be found in the baking section of most health food stores, and is sometimes sold under the "Fruit Fresh" or "Produce Protection" names. Always check ingredient listings for contents.

Variation

Substitute your favorite jam for the raspberry.

Caution

Do not let whipping cream come to a boil; it will result in a grainy truffle.

1. Line an 8-inch square pan with foil. Grease with butter and set aside.

2. Melt the white chocolate in a 1 quart oven proof saucepan using the oven method described on page 245. Meanwhile, heat the cream in a heavy 1 quart saucepan over low heat until it begins to steam; do NOT allow it to boil. Remove from heat and let sit until slightly cooled, but still very warm.

3. Immediately pour melted white chocolate into a medium sized mixing bowl. Pour warm cream over chocolate, and beat with an electric mixer until well-blended (about 30 seconds). Add citric acid and jam, and stir just until jam is mixed in. Spread mixture evenly into prepared pan. Refrigerate 2 hours, until firm.

4. Remove candy from pan using foil edges to lift. Transfer to a flat cutting surface. Remove foil and use a sharp edge to cut into 1 inch squares (8 rows by 8 rows). Transfer to mini candy cups.

5. Store between sheets of wax paper in a closed container in the refrigerator for up to 4 weeks. Do not freeze or store at room temperature.

Virginia City Truffles

Our version of the peanut butter truffle doubles as a power bar, full of granola and peanut butter!

1. Line a baking sheet with wax paper, and set aside. Break 4 oz. almond bark into pieces, and place in a medium sized microwave safe bowl. Microwave on HIGH 90 seconds. Stir well. Microwave in 15 second intervals, stirring after each, until mixture is creamy and smooth.

2. Immediately add peanut butter, and stir until smooth. Add sugar, vanilla and cereal. Stir until well combined.

3. Use a small cookie scoop to form mixture into 1 inch balls. Set aside at room temperature for 30 minutes. Melt the dark chocolate in a 1 quart oven proof saucepan, using the oven method described on page 245. Dip each truffle into the melted chocolate, then shake off excess. Place on prepared baking sheet to set (about 2 hours). If desired, transfer to mini candy cups.

4. Store between sheets of wax paper in a closed container in the refrigerator for up to 4 weeks. Do not freeze or store at room temperature.

6 oz. Vanilla Flavored Almond Bark Coating
3/4 Cup Crunchy Peanut Butter
1/2 Cup Powdered Sugar
1 Tbls. Vanilla
3/4 Cup Crushed Granola Cereal without Raisins

12 oz. Dark Chocolate

Mini Candy Cups (Optional)

tip
For test purposes, we used Quaker Brand 100% Natural Granola. To crush granola, place in a resealable plastic bag, and roll over several times with a rolling pin for crushed pieces (see page 240).

tip
For test purposes, we used JIF Brand Extra Crunchy Peanut Butter. To measure peanut butter, pour 3/4 cup water in a 2 cup sized measuring cup. Then, add peanut butter until the water line reaches the 1 1/2 cup line. Drain the water and add the peanut butter to the recipe.

Storage
Note container in photo; perfect for storing chocolates. It is actually a bin used for storing arts and crafts, and can be purchased at your local craft supply or discount store.

Caution
Let balls sit at room temperature at least 30 minutes before dipping into chocolate; otherwise, condensation occurs and will cause chocolate to separate.

☑ Favorite

A chocolate drizzle tops this elegant mint truffle.

1/3 Cup Heavy Whipping Cream
1/4 Cup Soft Butter
10 oz. Pkg. Creme de Menthe Baking Chips
1/2 Cup Semisweet Chocolate Chips
12 oz. Vanilla Flavored Almond Bark Coating
3 Drops Green Food Coloring
6 oz. Chocolate Flavored Candy Coating

Mini Candy Cups (Optional)

tip

For test purposes, we used Andes Brand Creme de Menthe Baking Chips.

tip

A plastic squeeze bottle can be used for squeezing melted chocolate in lines or patterns over candies. If the glaze becomes too thick, microwave it inside the bottle for 15 second intervals at 30% power.

1. Line a baking sheet with wax paper and set aside. Combine whipping cream and butter in a heavy 2-quart saucepan. Cook and stir over medium low heat, until butter is melted. Add chips and continue cooking, gently stirring with a wooden spoon, until melted and smooth. Refrigerate (do not cover) for 1 hour 30 minutes, until firm.

2. Working quickly, and using a small cookie scoop, drop by FLAT (no overflow mixture on scoop) scoopfuls onto prepared baking sheet. If mixture becomes sticky, dust the inside of the cookie scoop with powdered sugar. Freeze truffles (uncovered) for 30 minutes.

3. Meanwhile, break almond bark into pieces, and place in a medium sized microwave safe bowl. Microwave on HIGH 60 seconds. Stir well. Microwave on HIGH 60 more seconds. Stir until smooth. Add food coloring and stir until smooth.

4. Dip each truffle into almond bark mixture, making sure to coat entire piece. Shake off excess, and place on baking sheet to cool and set. Melt chocolate coating (same as almond bark instructions above). Drizzle chocolate over truffles. Refrigerate until set (about 1 hour). Transfer to mini candy cups.

5. Store between sheets of wax paper in an airtight container in the refrigerator for up to 4 weeks. Do not store at room temperature or freeze.

Shelby's Praline Candy Truffles

Low Sugar   ✓ Favorite

These elegant dark chocolate praline truffles should be reserved for a special occasion!

1. Line a baking sheet with wax paper and set aside. Combine chocolate and whipping cream in a 2 quart oven proof saucepan. Melt the mixture using the oven method described on page 245. Check that chocolate is completely melted before removing from oven. Remove from oven, and whisk until mixture is smooth.

2. Whisk in butter and liqueur, and let stand 20 minutes. Beat mixture in pan with an electric mixture for 3-4 minutes, or until mixture forms soft peaks (do NOT over beat). Use a small cookie scoop to drop heaping scoopfuls onto prepared baking sheet. Cover and chill at least 2 hours. Remove from refrigerator 30 minutes prior to coating with pecan mixture.

3. Praline Pecans: Preheat oven to 350˚. Lightly grease a round cake pan with butter, and set aside. Mix all ingredients in a small bowl. Spread in prepared pan. Bake for 20 minutes, or until coating appears slightly crystallized, stirring once. Remove from oven, and spread out on a foil lined baking sheet. Use fingers to break apart clumps of nuts while still warm. Cool completely.

4. Roll balls in Praline Pecans. Make sure to coat all sides of the truffle. If desired, transfer to mini candy cups.

5. Store between sheets of wax paper in an airtight container in the refrigerator for up to 2 weeks, or in the freezer up to 6 weeks. Do not store at room temperature.

12 oz. Dark Chocolate
1/3 Cup Whipping Cream
3 Tbls. Soft Butter, Cut Up
2 Tbls. Almond Liqueur

Praline Pecans:
1 1/2 Cups Finely Chopped Pecans
1/3 Cup Packed Brown Sugar
2 Tbls. Whipping Cream

Mini Candy Cups (Optional)

tip
Use a nut mill to finely chop pecans (see page 240), or purchase finely chopped pecans in the baking section of your local supermarket.

tip
For test purposes, we used Hershey's Brand Special Dark Chocolate Bars, and Amaretto Brand Almond Liqueur.

Variation
These truffles can be made with white chocolate instead of the dark.

The No Fuss Gift That Plays On, And On . . .

Visit your local dollar store for inexpensive candy tins.
Assemble a batch of "Bear Lake Bridge Mix"
on Page 78.
Attach to the latest and greatest board game,
wrap up as a gift, and surprise
the game lover(s) in your life!

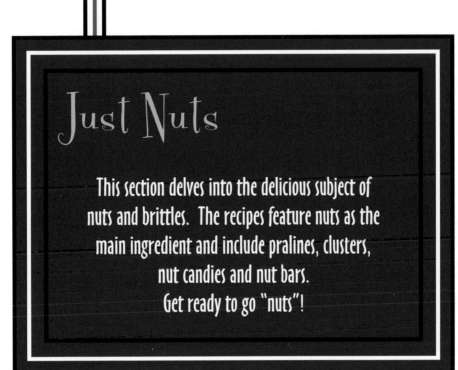

Just Nuts

This section delves into the delicious subject of
nuts and brittles. The recipes feature nuts as the
main ingredient and include pralines, clusters,
nut candies and nut bars.
Get ready to go "nuts"!

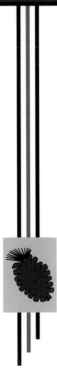

Conifer Nut Candy

2 Cups Glazed Nuts

✓ Favorite   🕐 Quick n' Easy

This glazed almond crunch candy is so incredible,
we suggest you double the recipe!

1/2 Cup Water
1 Cup Sugar
2 Cups Whole Raw Almonds

tip

Due to their high fat content, nuts can quickly turn rancid. Keep nut meats in the freezer until ready to use (up to one year). For best results, we recommend you store all finished nut recipes in the refrigerator (not at room temperature or in the freezer).

Caution

As the nuts begin to caramelize, you will hear a loud "popping" sound. This is simply the sound of roasting nuts.

1. Set aside an ungreased 10x15x1 inch jelly roll pan. In a heavy dark coated 2 quart skillet, combine water and sugar. Place over high heat, and stir with a wooden spoon until the mixture comes to a boil.

2. Add the almonds and stir continuously. Reduce heat to medium, and stir almonds until the mixture foams and turns to sugar. Continue stirring for 10 minutes, then reduce heat to medium-low. Stir constantly as almonds become coated with sugar (will appear white in color); sugar will then begin to remelt, and caramelize on the almonds. Continue stirring until all nuts have turned a nice deep brown color (all white coating on nuts will have disappeared, about 15 minutes).

3. Remove from heat, and turn out onto baking pan. Using 2 forks, immediately separate almonds into single nuts. Cool completely.

4. Store in a tightly sealed canning jar in the refrigerator for up to 2 months. Do not store at room temperature or freeze. Serve at room temperature.

Sedgwick's Sesame Bites

You're probably familiar with the sesame crunch candy sold in Chinese markets; we've added almonds for a special touch!

✓
Favorite

1. Line an 8-inch square pan with foil leaving a 2-inch overhang on 2 sides. Grease with butter and set aside.

2. Melt the butter in a 2 quart heavy saucepan over low heat. Watch carefully so it does not burn. Add the sugar, and raise the heat to medium. Stir constantly with a wooden spoon until the sugar dissolves, and the syrup comes to a boil. Add seeds and almonds. Continue to occasionally stir, about 8-10 minutes. Butter will begin to separate from mixture, as it turns brown. As soon as the mixture is a deep golden brown, pour excess butter off the top into a grease container (to later discard).

3. Immediately pour the hot candy mixture into the prepared pan, and spread as evenly as possible with the wooden spoon. Allow the candy to cool for about 10 minutes. Using a sharp edge, score into 36 pieces (6 rows by 6 rows). Cool completely, then score again. Remove candy from pan using foil edges to lift. Transfer to a flat cutting surface. Remove foil and break into pieces along scored lines.

4. Store between sheets of wax paper in an airtight container, or tightly sealed canning jar in the refrigerator for up to 1 month. Do not freeze or store at room temperature.

1/2 Cup Soft Butter
1 Cup Sugar
1/2 Cup White Sesame Seeds
1/2 Cup Sliced Almonds

tip

Using a wooden spoon is essential; the handle won't get HOT, and can be held in your hand during the entire stirring process.

tip

If sugar crystals form inside the pan, wipe down with a damp paper towel.

Caution

Watch mixture carefully after you add the nuts, so it does not burn.

This spectacular walnut brittle has a heavenly butter taste!

1/2 Cup Butter
1/4 Cup Water
1 Tbls. Honey
1 Cup Packed Brown Sugar
3/4 Cup Finely Chopped
     Walnuts

tip

Due to their high fat content, nuts can quickly turn rancid. Keep nut meats in the freezer until ready to use (up to one year). For best results, we recommend you store all finished nut recipes in the refrigerator (not at room temperature or in the freezer).

tip

Perform the candy thermometer test on page 246 to determine the proper cooking temperature at your altitude.

1. Line an 8-inch square baking pan with foil, leaving a 2-inch overhang on 2 sides. Grease with butter and set aside. Use a nut mill to finely chop walnuts (see page 240).

2. In a heavy 2 quart saucepan, combine butter, water, honey and brown sugar. Place over high heat, and stir with a wooden spoon until mixture comes to a boil. If sugar crystals are present, wipe down sides of the pan with a damp paper towel. Turn the heat down to medium high, and watch mixture closely.

3. Cook mixture to 280˚ (soft-crack stage). Immediately stir in walnuts and pour into prepared pan. Cool at room temperature (about 1 hour). Remove candy from pan using foil edges to lift. Remove foil, and break candy into desired sized pieces.

4. Store between sheets of wax paper in an airtight tin, or tightly sealed canning jar in the refrigerator for up to 6 weeks. Do not store at room temperature or freeze. Serve at room temperature.

5 Cups Nut Medley

Quick n' Easy   Favorite

Just Nuts

Northglenn Nut Medley

*This combination tastes just like the cinnamon roasted nuts
at the state fair - - with an added touch of chocolate!*

1. Preheat oven to 265°. Grease a 10 x 15 x 1 inch jelly roll pan with nonstick cooking spray. Set aside.

2. In a large mixing bowl, combine egg white and water, and beat until frothy, but not stiff. Add nuts, and stir until well coated. In a small measuring cup, combine sugar, salt and cinnamon, and stir until well combined. Pour over nut mixture and toss to coat well. Spread nut mixture evenly in prepared pan.

3. Bake for 1 hour 20 minutes, stirring every 20 minutes. Remove from oven, and place on a wire rack to cool completely. In a large bowl, combine nut mixture and chocolate pieces.

4. Store in an airtight tin or tightly sealed canning jar, in the refrigerator for up to 2 months. Do not store at room temperature or freeze. Serve at room temperature.

1 Egg White at Room
    Temperature
2 Tsp. Water
2 Cups Whole Almonds
1 Cup Whole Cashews
1 Cup Pecan Halves
2/3 Cup Sugar
1/2 Tsp. Salt
1 Tsp. Cinnamon
1 Cup Candy Coated Milk
    Chocolate Pieces

tip

Due to their high fat content, nuts can quickly turn rancid. Keep nut meats in the freezer until ready to use (up to one year). For best results, we recommend you store all finished nut recipes in the refrigerator (not at room temperature or in the freezer).

tip

Remove egg from the refrigerator 20-30 minutes before candy making. Remember, eggs separate more easily when they are COLD.

Quantities Vary

✓ Favorite   Quick n' Easy

*Gather around the game table with this
easy to assemble candy and nut gift mix.*

Roasted and Salted Peanuts
Roasted and Salted Cashews

Brand Name Candies:
M&M's, All Varieties
Hershey's Kisses, All Varieties
Whoppers Malted Milk Balls
Nestle Buncha Crunch
Reese's Pieces
Sugar Babies
Brach's French Burnt Peanuts
Ferrara Pan Boston Baked
   Beans
Junior Caramels
Hershey's Milk Duds
Candy Corn
Chocolate Stars
Butter Mints (Not Pastel Mints)
Nestle Raisinets
Rolo Chewy Caramels
Etc., Etc., Etc.

1. Combine nuts and desired candies together in a large bowl.
Stir with a large spoon to combine. It is best to have a ratio of
2 1/2 times the amount of candy to nuts (i.e. 5 cups candy to
2 cups nuts).

2. Scoop mixture into smaller containers for gift giving, or
leave in a large container for group gatherings.

3. Store in an airtight tin, or tightly sealed canning jar, in the
refrigerator for up to 4 weeks. Do not freeze or store at room
temperature. Serve at room temperature.

tip
*The list of possible candy
combinations is endless.
Choose candies that suit your
individual taste, and go well
with nuts.*

Caution
*Avoid fruit flavored candies,
as the taste does not mix well
with chocolate and nuts.*

Bedrock Bark

A sugar n' spice nut mixture pressed into creamy almond bark; there are enough nuts left over for the bridge crowd!

1. Preheat oven to 275°. Grease a 10 x 15 x1 inch jelly roll pan with nonstick cooking spray. Line a 9 x 13 inch pan with foil, leaving a 2-inch overhang on 2 sides. Grease with butter. Break almond bark into pieces, and place in a medium sized microwave safe bowl along with half n' half. Set aside.

2. In a large mixing bowl, beat the egg white until foamy. Add butter and stir. Add all the nuts, and stir to combine.
In a large measuring cup, combine sugar, cornstarch, cinnamon, allspice, nutmeg and salt. Stir until well combined. Sprinkle over nut mixture, and stir until nuts are well coated. Spread evenly in jelly roll pan. Bake 45 minutes, or until toasted and crisp, stirring every 15 minutes. Cool completely on wire rack.

3. As soon as nuts have cooled, microwave almond bark mixture on HIGH 90 seconds. Stir well. Microwave on HIGH 60 more seconds. Stir again. Spread evenly into the bottom of the foil lined pan. Let cool 3 minutes. Sprinkle 2 cups of the nut mixture, evenly over the almond bark. Use a spatula, to lightly press nuts into bark.

4. Wait about 20 minutes, and use a cleaver or heavy duty knife to score into 35 rectangular pieces (7 rows by 5 rows). Cool completely, then score again. Remove candy from pan using foil edges to lift. Transfer to a flat cutting surface. Remove foil and break into pieces along scored lines.

5. Store bark between sheets of wax paper in an airtight container in the refrigerator for up to 1 month. Store nuts in a tightly sealed canning jar in the refrigerator for up to 1 month. Do not freeze or store at room temperature.

24 oz. Vanilla Flavored Almond Bark Coating
2 Tbls. Half n' Half (No Substitutions)
1 Egg White Slightly Beaten
2 Tbls. Melted Butter
1 Cup Dry Roasted or Cocktail Peanuts
1 Cup Chopped Walnuts
1/2 Cup Chopped Cashews
1/2 Cup Slivered Almonds
1/2 Cup Pecan Halves
1/2 Cup Dry Roasted Sunflower Kernels
3/4 Cup Sugar
2 Tbls. Cornstarch
1 1/2 Tsp. Cinnamon
1/2 Tsp. Allspice
1/2 Tsp. Nutmeg
1/4 Tsp. Salt

tip
Remove egg from the refrigerator 20-30 minutes before candy making. Remember, eggs separate more easily when they are COLD.

Caution
Nuts can become rancid if stored for a long time at room temperature. For best results, refrigerate or freeze.

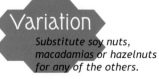

Variation
Substitute soy nuts, macadamias or hazelnuts for any of the others.

√
Favorite

*Sour cream gives these nuts
a creamy texture, and a slightly tangy taste.*

1 Cup Packed Brown Sugar
1/2 Cup Sugar
2/3 Cup Sour Cream
1 1/2 Tsp. Vanilla
1 Cup Toasted Pecan Halves
1 Cup Toasted Whole Almonds
1 Cup Toasted Walnut Halves

tip

Due to their high fat content, nuts can quickly turn rancid. Keep nut meats in the freezer until ready to use (up to one year). For best results, we recommend you store all finished nut recipes in the refrigerator (not at room temperature or in the freezer).

tip

Perform the candy thermometer test on page 246 to determine the proper cooking temperature at your altitude.

1. To toast nuts, arrange on a foil-lined baking sheet in a 350° oven for 8-10 minutes, stirring 2 or 3 times, until desired flavor is reached. Cool completely. Grease a baking sheet with nonstick cooking spray and set aside.

2. In a heavy 2-quart saucepan, combine sugars with sour cream. Place over medium heat, and stir constantly with a wooden spoon until mixture comes to a boil. If sugar crystals are present, wipe down sides of the pan with a damp paper towel.

3. Cook mixture, stirring continually, to 238° (soft-ball stage, takes 15-20 minutes; mixture will turn a medium golden brown color). Remove from heat, and let stand 3 minutes. Stir in vanilla until well mixed, then add nuts and mix until well coated. Turn mixture onto prepared baking sheet, and with 2 forks, break apart into clusters. Cool Completely.

4. Store between sheets of wax paper in an airtight tin, or tightly sealed canning jar in the refrigerator for up to 6 weeks. Do not store at room temperature or freeze. Serve at room temperature.

Caution
Be sure to continually stir mixture while boiling, or it will easily burn.

Variation
Try just one type of nut in this recipe instead of three.

Poncha Springs Nut Candy

1 1/2 Pounds

Quick n' Easy   Favorite

These caramelized pecans can be made into a brittle, or individual candied nuts, depending upon the amount of sugar you add to the recipe.

1. Preheat oven to 300˚. Spread pecans on a foil lined baking sheet, and bake for 8 minutes, stirring every 2 minutes. Turn oven off, and leave nuts inside, with oven door ajar. Grease a baking sheet with butter and set aside.

2. While nuts are crisping, place sugar in a medium-sized skillet over medium-high heat. With a wooden spoon, stir sugar until it melts, and turns into golden syrup (about 6-7 minutes). Remove nuts from oven, and add to hot syrup, stirring until nuts are well-coated. Pour out onto prepared baking sheet to cool. When completely cooled, break into pieces.

3. Store between sheets of wax paper in an airtight tin, or tightly sealed canning jar in the refrigerator for up to 6 weeks. Do not store at room temperature or freeze. Serve at room temperature.

2 1/4 Cups Pecan Halves
2 Cups Sugar

Caution
Sugar syrup is HOT; it will burn your skin if you touch it.

Variation
Decrease the amount of sugar in the recipe to 1 1/2 cups, and you will have individual candied nuts; great for sprinkling on a special salad!

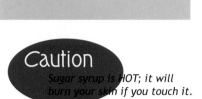

√ Favorite   Quick n' Easy

The slight cinnamon flavor in these sugar crusted walnuts is irresistible . . . especially when served warm.

2 1/2 Cups Walnut Halves
1/2 Cup Water
1 Cup Sugar
1 Tsp. Cinnamon
1 Tsp. Salt
2 Tsp. Vanilla

tip

When cooking candy, always place the liquids in the pan first, then the sugar. This will minimize sugar crystals from forming on the inside of the cooking pan.

tip

Nuts are especially good served warm; before serving, heat in a 250˚ oven for 5-7 minutes.

1. Preheat oven to 350˚. Spread walnuts on a foil lined baking sheet. Bake for 5 minutes. Turn oven off, leaving nuts in warm oven. Line another baking sheet with wax paper and set aside.

2. In a heavy 2 quart saucepan, combine water, sugar, cinnamon and salt. Cook on high heat, and stir with a wooden spoon, until mixture comes to a boil. If sugar crystals are present, wipe down sides of pan with a damp paper towel.

3. Turn heat down to medium-high, and stirring occasionally, cook syrup to 238˚ (soft-ball stage). Remove from heat, and with a wooden spoon, beat 1 minute, or until mixture becomes creamy. Add vanilla and warm nuts, and stir until well-coated. Spread on prepared baking sheet to cool. Using 2 forks, separate walnuts. Let cool completely.

4. Store in an airtight tin, or tightly sealed canning jar in the refrigerator for up to 2 months. Do not store at room temperature or freeze. Serve at room temperature.

Caution

Perform the candy thermometer test on page 246 to determine the proper cooking temperature at your altitude.

36 Toffee Squares

Low Sugar   Quick n' Easy   Favorite

Trevor's Town Toffee Bites

*If you have 5 minutes to spare - - you can stir up
a fabulous, crunchy, almond butter toffee!*

1. Line an 8 inch square pan with foil leaving a 2 inch overhang on 2 sides. Grease with butter and set aside.

2. Butter the inside of a 2 quart heavy saucepan. Melt 1/2 cup butter in the same pan over medium heat. Add sugar and corn syrup. Stir constantly with a wooden spoon over medium high heat, until mixture comes to a boil. Continue to cook and stir, until mixture turns golden brown (about 4 minutes). Remove from heat, and stir in almonds. Quickly pour into prepared pan, and spread evenly to all edges.

3. Let pan cool at room temperature for 5-7 minutes, or until mixture is still very warm, but firm to the touch. Remove candy from pan using foil edges to lift. Use a cleaver or heavy duty knife to immediately cut into 36 squares (6 rows by 6 rows). Candy will fully harden once it has cooled completely.

4. Store between sheets of wax paper in an airtight tin container or tightly sealed canning jar in the refrigerator for up to 6 weeks. Do not store at room temperature or freeze. Serve at room temperature.

| 1/2 Cup Soft Butter |
| 1/2 Cup Sugar |
| 1 1/2 Tbls. Light Corn Syrup |
| 1 Cup Sliced Almonds |

tip

When cooking candy, always place the liquids in the pan first (in this case melted butter). This will help eliminate sugar crystals from forming on the inside of the cooking pan.

tip

Due to their high fat content, nuts can quickly turn rancid. Keep nut meats in the freezer until ready to use (up to one year). For best results, we recommend you store all finished nut recipes in the refrigerator (not at room temperature or in the freezer).

The addition of butter to this recipe creates a brittle that is deep golden brown in color and irresistible to the taste buds!

1 1/2 Tsp. Baking Soda
1 Tsp. Water
1 Tsp. Vanilla
1 Cup Water
1 1/2 Cups Sugar
1 Cup Light Corn Syrup
4 Tbls. Soft Butter
1 Lb. Shelled and Unroasted Peanuts (Spanish with Skins)

tip

When cooking candy, always place the liquids in the pan first, then the sugar. This will minimize sugar crystals from forming on the inside of the cooking pan.

tip

Perform the candy thermometer test on page 246 to determine the proper cooking temperature at your altitude.

1. Grease 2 large baking sheets with butter and set aside. Combine the soda, 1 tsp. water and vanilla in a small cup. Set aside.

2. Butter the inside of a heavy 3 quart saucepan. Combine 1 cup water, sugar and corn syrup. Stir with a wooden spoon over medium high heat, until sugar is dissolved. If sugar crystals are visible on inside of pan, wipe down with a damp paper towel. When mixture comes to a boil, lower heat to medium, and cook, stirring occasionally, to 238° (soft-ball stage).

3. Immediately stir in butter and peanuts. Cook, stirring constantly, to 300°(hard-crack stage; about 14-16 minutes). Immediately remove from heat, and stir in soda mixture until combined. Pour half the candy mixture onto each prepared baking sheet, and quickly spread to 1/4 inch thickness (thinness is the key to brittleness). Cool completely, then break into pieces.

4. Store between sheets of wax paper in an airtight tin, or tightly sealed canning jar in the refrigerator for up to 6 weeks. Do not freeze or store at room temperature. Serve at room temperature.

Caution
Watch your candy mixture closely; it can easily burn near the 300° mark.

Lake City Brittle

A mouth-watering brittle that features a base of candied macadamia and pecan nuts, topped with toasted coconut.

1. To toast the coconut, preheat oven to 350˚. Spread the coconut in a single layer on a foil lined baking sheet. Bake for 8-10 minutes, stirring twice, until light golden brown. The coconut will become crisper as it cools. Cool completely. Chop pecans with a chef's knife on a cutting board. Combine soda, water and vanilla in a small cup. Set all items aside.

2. Grease a baking sheet with nonstick cooking spray, and sprinkle toasted coconut in a 12-inch diameter circle on sheet. In a heavy 2 quart saucepan, combine corn syrup and sugar. Cook over medium heat, stirring constantly with a wooden spoon, to 240˚ (soft-ball stage; about 2 minutes). If sugar crystals are visible inside pan, wipe down with a damp paper towel.

3. Immediately stir in nuts and butter. Cook and stir occasionally, until the mixture reaches 300˚ (hard-crack stage). Immediately remove from heat, and stir in soda and vanilla mixture, until well combined. Quickly pour nut mixture over the coconut, making sure it spreads to all edges. Let cool completely, then break into pieces.

4. Store between sheets of wax paper in an airtight tin, or tightly sealed canning jar in the refrigerator for up to 6 weeks. Do not freeze or store at room temperature. Serve at room temperature.

1 Cup Sweetened Flaked
   Coconut, Toasted
1 Tsp. Baking Soda
1 Tsp. Water
1 Tsp. Vanilla
1/2 Cup Light Corn Syrup
1 Cup Sugar
1 Cup Whole Roasted
   Macadamia Nuts
   (About 3 oz.)
3/4 Cup Coarsely Chopped
   Pecans
2 Tbls. Soft Butter

tip

Due to their high fat content, nuts can quickly turn rancid. Keep nut meats in the freezer until ready to use (up to one year). For best results, we recommend you store all finished nut recipes in the refrigerator (not at room temperature or in the freezer).

tip

When cooking candy, always place liquids in the pan first, then the sugar. This will minimize sugar crystals from forming on the inside of the cooking pan.

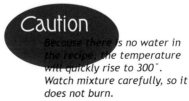

Caution

Because there is no water in the recipe, the temperature will quickly rise to 300˚. Watch mixture carefully, so it does not burn.

Burlington's Nut Snappers

1/2 Pound

Quick n' Easy

A golden mixed nut brittle that is cooked in the microwave oven, and ready in 15 minutes!

1/2 Cup Sugar
1/2 Cup Light Corn Syrup
3/4 Cup Salted Mixed Nuts
2 Tbls. Butter
1 Tsp. Vanilla
1/2 Tsp. Baking Soda

Variation

Substitute peanuts for a more traditional tasty treat!

Caution

Check that the measuring cup you use is heavy-duty glass that withstands high temperatures. It must be free from cracks and chips, and labelled "microwave safe", or it will shatter during cooking.

1. Grease a baking sheet with butter and set aside. In a microwave-safe 4-cup glass measuring cup, combine sugar and corn syrup. Microwave uncovered, on HIGH for 5 minutes, stirring twice.

2. Stir in nuts and butter. Microwave mixture, uncovered, on HIGH for 1 more minute. Stir mixture again. Then, microwave on HIGH, in 15 second increments, for up to 30 seconds, or until mixture turns golden (watch carefully; mixture continues to cook and becomes darker when removed from microwave).

3. Stir in vanilla and baking soda. Immediately pour onto prepared baking sheet. Spread into a thin layer. Cool completely, then break into pieces.

4. Store between sheets of wax paper in an airtight tin, or tightly sealed canning jar in the refrigerator for up to 6 weeks. Do not freeze or store at room temperature. Serve at room temperature.

Bunny's Brittle Bars

Favorite

These bars resemble the taste of peanut brittle - - with a creamy, caramel coated topping.

1. Preheat oven to 350°. Grease a 9 x 13 inch glass baking dish with nonstick cooking spray and set aside.

2. Combine all crust ingredients in a medium sized mixing bowl, and stir until well combined. Using fingers, press evenly in bottom of prepared pan. Bake 12-14 minutes, or until golden brown.

3. Remove from oven, and immediately sprinkle peanuts and chocolate chips over warm base. In a small, microwave safe bowl, combine caramels and half n' half. Microwave on HIGH 1 minute 30 seconds, stirring every 30 seconds, or until smooth. Add flour and stir until well mixed. Drizzle caramel evenly over chocolate chips and peanuts. Return to the oven, and bake 15-17 minutes, or until topping is set and golden brown. Cool completely on wire rack.

4. When bars have completely cooled, use a sharp edge to cut into 48 bars (8 rows by 6 rows).

5. Bars stay fresher if left uncut until served. Cover pan tightly with foil, and store at room temperature up to 3 days, or in the refrigerator up to 10 days. Do not freeze.

Crust:
1 1/2 Cups Flour
3/4 Cup Packed Brown Sugar
3/4 Tsp. Baking Soda
1/2 Tsp. Salt
3/4 Cup Melted Butter

Topping:
1 1/2 Cups Cocktail or Dry
    Roasted Peanuts
1 Cup Milk Chocolate Chips
7 oz. Caramels (About
    26 Pieces)
1 1/2 Tbls. Half n' Half
1 Tbls. Flour

tip
Melting the butter before adding to crust ingredients makes for a smoother textured base.

Variation
Try adding 1/2 Cup Butterscotch Flavored Chips to the topping.

24 Nut Bars

☑
Favorite

If you're in a rush, you can still whip up these tasty, nutty, double chocolate treats!

1 Cup Packed Brown Sugar
1 Cup Soft Butter
1 Tsp. Vanilla
1 Egg Yolk
2 Cups Flour
1/2 Tsp. Salt
6 oz. Semisweet Chocolate Chips
6 oz. Premier White Baking Chips
12 oz. Can Salted Mixed Nuts, Chopped

Below 3,500 Feet
Oven: 350˚
Flour: Subtract 2 Tbls.

Caution

Do not use a metal pan for this recipe; it will result in a dry bar.

1. Preheat oven to 375˚.

2. Microwave the butter in a small microwave safe bowl, covered, at 40% power for 45 seconds. In a large sized mixing bowl, combine brown sugar, butter, vanilla and egg yolk. Beat until creamy, scraping sides of bowl often (about 1-2 minutes). Stir in flour and salt. Using fingers, evenly press mixture into ungreased 9 x 13 inch glass baking dish. Bake 22 minutes, or until golden brown.

3. Remove from oven, and immediately sprinkle chips evenly over baked layer. Sprinkle nuts on top. Using a spatula, gently compress nuts into chips. Cool completely.

4. Use a sharp edge to cut into 24 bars (6 rows by 4 rows).

5. Bars stay fresher if left uncut until served. Cover pan tightly with foil, and store at room temperature up to 3 days, or in the refrigerator up to 10 days. To freeze, cut bars and wrap individually in plastic food wrap. Transfer to an airtight container, and freeze up to 4 months.

tip

Due to their high fat content, nuts can quickly turn rancid. Keep nut meats in the freezer until ready to use (up to one year). For best results, we recommend you store all finished nut recipes in the refrigerator (not at room temperature or in the freezer).

Variation

If you don't like the combination of mixed nuts, substitute your favorite nut.

Pudding mix enhances the creamy texture of these traditional praline candies.

1. Coarsely chop pecans with a chef's knife on a cutting board. Line a baking sheet with wax paper, and set aside.

2. In a heavy 2-quart saucepan, combine milk, pudding mix, sugars and butter. Cook over medium heat, and stir with a wooden spoon, until mixture comes to a boil. If sugar crystals are present, wipe down sides of the pan with a damp paper towel.

3. Cook, stirring occasionally until mixture reaches 234° (soft-ball stage; about 10 minutes). Remove from heat. See Caution Below. Add pecans and stir ONLY 30 seconds until mixture looks creamy and is slightly thickened. Immediately drop by tablespoonfuls onto prepared baking sheet. Cool completely.

4. Store between sheets of wax paper in an airtight tin, or tightly sealed canning jar in the refrigerator for up to 6 weeks. Do not freeze or store at room temperature. Serve at room temperature.

3/4 Cup Evaporated Milk
1 (3.5 oz.) Pkg. Cook and Stir
    Butterscotch Pudding
1 Cup Sugar
1/2 Cup Packed Brown Sugar
2 Tbls. Soft Butter
1 1/4 Cups Coarsely Chopped
    Pecans

tip

Perform the candy thermometer test on page 246 to determine the proper cooking temperature at your altitude.

Variation

For chocolate pralines, use chocolate pudding mix in place of the butterscotch.

Caution

Once you remove candy mixture from heat, do not over stir; it will crystallize and turn to sugar.

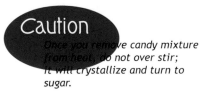

Summit City Nut Clusters

Just Nuts

✓ Favorite   🕐 Quick n' Easy

A peanut and almond nut cluster with a chocolate base,
and a marbled white chocolate topping.

12 oz. Dark Chocolate
3/4 Cup Chopped Dry Roasted
    or Cocktail Peanuts
3/4 Cup Sliced, Toasted
    Almonds
2 oz. White Chocolate

tip

Due to their high fat content, nuts can quickly turn rancid. Keep nut meats in the freezer until ready to use (up to one year). For best results, we recommend you store all finished nut recipes in the refrigerator (not at room temperature or in the freezer).

tip

For test purposes, we used Hershey's Brand Special Dark Chocolate Candy Bars.

1. To toast almonds, place sliced nuts in a single layer on a foil-lined baking sheet in a 350˚ oven for 7-8 minutes, stirring 2 or 3 times, until desired flavor is reached. Cool completely. Line baking sheets with wax paper and set aside.

2. Melt the chocolates separately in 1 quart oven proof saucepans, using the oven method described on page 245. Remove from oven. Set the white chocolate aside. Add the nuts to the dark chocolate, and stir until well coated. Drop by large spoonfuls onto the prepared baking sheets.

3. Immediately drizzle a small amount of the white chocolate atop each cluster, and swirl gently with a toothpick to create a marbled effect (see photo). Let set (about 2 hours).

4. Do NOT cover the candies until the chocolate has set and dried. Store between sheets of wax paper in an airtight tin, plastic craft container with lid, cardboard box with lid, or foil covered container. Keep in a cool, dry, dark place (i.e. closed kitchen cabinet), for up to 3 weeks. Do not refrigerate or freeze.

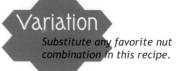

Variation

Substitute any favorite nut combination in this recipe.

Quick n' Easy   Favorite

Just Nuts

Highlands Ranch Peanut Clusters

*These delightful clusters take just a few minutes,
and yield candy shoppe quality candies!*

1. Line a baking sheet with wax paper and set aside.

2. Melt the chocolate in a 2 quart oven proof saucepan using the oven method described on page 245. Let cool 5 minutes.

3. Add nuts, and stir gently until well coated. Drop by tablespoonfuls onto prepared baking sheet. Let set (about 2 hours).

4. Do NOT cover the candies until the chocolate has set and dried. Store between sheets of wax paper in an airtight tin, plastic craft container with lid, cardboard box with lid, or foil covered container. Keep in a cool, dry, dark place (i.e. closed kitchen cabinet), for up to 6 weeks. Do not refrigerate or freeze.

24 oz. Milk Chocolate Bars
24 oz. Cocktail or Dry
     Roasted Peanuts

tip

For testing purposes we used 3 (8 oz.) Hershey's Brand Chocolate Bars.

Variation

Any type nut can be substituted for the peanuts. Use equal amounts of chocolate and toasted nuts.

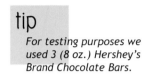

√ Favorite

Quick n' Easy

*It will take no time at all to present your friends
with a dish of these luscious pecan delights!*

**3 Cups Coarsely Chopped
Toasted Pecans
12 oz. Milk Chocolate**

tip

*For test purposes, we used
2 (8 oz.) Hershey's Milk
Chocolate Bars.*

1. Line a baking sheet with wax paper and set aside. Chop pecans with a chef's knife on a cutting board (see page 240). To toast, transfer to a foil-lined baking sheet in a 350° oven for 5-8 minutes, stirring occasionally, or until golden brown. Cool completely.

2. Melt chocolate in a 2 quart oven proof saucepan using the oven method described on page 245. Remove from oven, let sit 3 minutes, then gently stir in the pecans. Mix until nuts are well coated. Drop by rounded tablespoonfuls onto prepared baking sheet. Let set (about 2 hours).

3. Do NOT cover the candies until the chocolate has set and dried. Store between sheets of wax paper in an airtight tin, plastic craft container with lid, cardboard box with lid, or foil covered container. Keep in a cool, dry, dark place (i.e. closed kitchen cabinet), for up to 6 weeks. Do not refrigerate or freeze.

Variation

*Any nut of choice can be substituted
for the pecans. Try substituting dark
chocolate for the milk chocolate.*

This candy is so easy to make - -
it's hard to believe it doesn't contain real caramel in the middle!

1. Line baking sheets with wax paper and set aside.

2. In a heavy, 2 quart saucepan, combine chopped peanuts, condensed milk, butter and vanilla. Cook and stir with a wooden spoon, over medium heat 10-12 minutes, or until mixture forms a ball around the spoon, and pulls away from the side of the pan. Remove from heat, and cool 10 minutes. Using a small cookie scoop, drop mixture by flat scoopfuls (no overflow candy), onto prepared baking sheets. Chill for 1 hour, then let sit at room temperature at least 30 minutes before dipping into the melted chocolate.

3. Melt the chocolate in a 1 quart oven proof saucepan using the oven method described on page 245. Dip each candy piece into the melted chocolate, and shake off excess. Immediately press a peanut half into the top of each candy, and place on wax paper lined baking sheets to set (about 2 hours).

4. Do NOT cover the candies until the chocolate has set and dried. Store between sheets of wax paper in an airtight tin, plastic craft container with lid, cardboard box with lid, or foil covered container. Keep in a cool, dry, dark place (i.e. closed kitchen cabinet), for up to 4 weeks. Do not refrigerate or freeze.

2 3/4 Cups Finely Chopped
   Dry Roasted or
   Cocktail Peanuts
14 oz. Can Sweetened
   Condensed Milk
2 Tbls. Soft Butter
1 Tsp. Vanilla
16 oz. Milk Chocolate
48 Half Peanuts (Dry Roasted
   or Cocktail)

Mini Candy Cups (Optional)

tip

To finely chop peanuts, place in a resealable plastic bag and roll over several times with a rolling pin for desired sized pieces (see page 240).

Favorite

This caramel nut filled cluster,
resembles a popular candy store treat.

1 Cup Walnut Halves
1 Cup Pecan Halves
1 Cup Whole Almonds
1 1/2 Cups Sugar
1 Cup Heavy Whipping Cream
1/2 Cup Light Corn Syrup

tip

Due to their high fat content, nuts can quickly turn rancid. Keep nut meats in the freezer until ready to use (up to one year). For best results, we recommend you store all finished nut recipes in the refrigerator (not at room temperature or in the freezer).

tip

Perform the candy thermometer test on page 246 to determine the proper cooking temperature at your altitude.

1. Place the nuts in a single layer on a foil lined baking sheet. Bake at 350° for 8-10 minutes, stirring after 4 minutes, until toasted and golden brown. Cool on a wire rack. Line an 8-inch square pan with foil, leaving a 2-inch overhang on 2 sides. Grease with butter and set aside.

2. In a heavy 3-quart saucepan, combine the sugar; cream and corn syrup. Bring to a boil over medium heat, stirring constantly with a wooden spoon. Stir in the toasted nuts. Reduce heat to medium low, and cook, without stirring, to 238° (soft-ball stage). Remove from heat, and stir mixture with a wooden spoon about 90 seconds, until creamy and thickened.

3. Quickly spread into prepared pan. Cool at room temperature for 1 hour. Cover loosely with foil, and refrigerate for 8 hours or overnight. Lift the candy out of the pan using foil edges to lift. Transfer to a cutting surface and use a cleaver or heavy duty knife to cut candy into desired sized pieces.

4. Store between sheets of wax paper in an airtight tin, or tightly sealed canning jar in the refrigerator for up to 6 weeks. Do not store at room temperature or freeze. Serve at room temperature.

Variation

Dip bottom of candies in milk chocolate; set upside down on wax paper sheets until set.

Coyote Cashew Bars

A bar that tastes like a cashew brittle and blonde brownie all in one!
One batch feeds a large crowd.

✓
Favorite

1. Heat oven to 350˚. Spray the bottom and sides of a 15 x 10 x 1 inch jelly roll pan with cooking spray. Set aside.

2. Crust: Mix brown sugar, butter, corn syrup, vanilla and egg in a large bowl with a spoon. Stir in flour and salt, and mix until well combined. Use a lightly floured rolling pin to spread evenly in prepared pan. Bake 18-20 minutes, or until light golden brown. Remove to wire rack.

3. Topping: Meanwhile, in a 2 quart saucepan over low heat, combine brown sugar and corn syrup. Stir constantly with a wooden spoon, until sugar is dissolved. Add butter and whipping cream. Stir and heat to boiling over medium heat. Boil 30 seconds, then remove from heat. Stir in vanilla and let mixture cool for 5 minutes.

4. Sprinkle cashews over warm crust. Drizzle topping mixture over cashews, coating evenly. Return to oven, and bake 15-20 minutes, or until light brown and set. Remove from oven and cool completely (about 1 hour). Use a sharp edge to cut into 60 bars (10 rows by 6 rows).

5. Store between sheets of wax paper in an airtight container in the refrigerator for up to 10 days. Do not freeze or store at room temperature. Serve at room temperature.

Crust:
1/2 Cup Packed Brown Sugar
2/3 Cup Soft Butter
1/2 Cup Light Corn Syrup
1 Tsp. Vanilla
1 Egg
2 Cups Flour
1/2 Tsp. Salt

Topping:
1/2 Cup Packed Brown Sugar
1/2 Cup Light Corn Syrup
1/3 Cup Soft Butter
1/3 Cup Heavy Whipping
    Cream
1 Tsp. Vanilla
2 Cups Cashew Halves and
    Pieces

Low Sugar

*The addition of a honey glazed topping,
enhances these scrumptious triple nut brownies!*

1 Cup Flour
1/2 Cup Sugar
1/3 Cup Melted Butter

Topping:
1/2 Cup Packed Brown Sugar
1/3 Cup Soft Butter
2 Tbls. Honey
1/3 Cup Heavy Whipping
    Cream
2/3 Cup Each Chopped Pecans,
    Walnuts and Sliced
    Almonds

1. Line a 9-inch square pan with foil, leaving a 2-inch overhang on 2 sides. Grease with butter and set aside. Preheat oven to 350˚.

2. In a small mixing bowl, combine flour, sugar and butter. Stir until well combined. Use fingers to press mixture evenly into prepared pan. Bake for 10 minutes. Remove from oven.

3. Topping: In a 2 quart heavy saucepan, combine the brown sugar, butter and honey. Heat and stir constantly over medium high heat, until mixture boils. Boil for 1 minute. Remove from heat, and stir in cream and nuts. Pour evenly over warm crust. Bake 16-20 minutes, or until surface is bubbly. Cool in pan on wire rack.

4. When completely cool, remove bars from pan using foil edges to lift. Transfer to a flat cutting surface. Remove foil and use a sharp edge to cut into 16 bars (4 rows by 4 rows).

5. Bars stay fresher if left uncut until served. Cover pan tightly with foil, and store at room temperature up to 3 days, or in the refrigerator up to 10 days. To freeze, cut bars and wrap individually in plastic food wrap. Transfer to an airtight container and freeze up to 4 months.

tip
To chop pecans and walnuts, place in a resealable plastic bag and roll over several times with a rolling pin for desired sized pieces (see page 240).

tip
Due to their high fat content, nuts can quickly turn rancid. Keep nut meats in the freezer until ready to use (up to one year).

Variation
Substitute your favorite nut combination.

Buffalo Creek Nut Balls

The longer these no-bake bourbon nut balls sit, the better they taste!

1. To toast pecans, place whole nuts in a single layer on a foil-lined baking sheet in a 350° oven for 8-10 minutes, stirring 2 or 3 times, until desired flavor is reached. Cool completely, then chop using a nut mill. Line a baking sheet with wax paper and set aside. To crush vanilla wafers, place in a resealable plastic bag, and run over several times with a rolling pin, until roughly crumbled (see page 240). Place in a large mixing bowl. Add the bourbon and stir. Allow mixture to soften (about 2 minutes).

2. Add powdered sugar, pecans, cocoa and corn syrup to vanilla wafer mixture. Stir until ingredients are well combined. Wrap mixture in plastic wrap, and chill for 30 minutes.

3. Use a small cookie scoop to form mixture into 1 inch balls, and place on prepared baking sheet.

4. Fill shaker with additional powdered sugar or cocoa powder. Generously sprinkle over candies to coat well.

5. Store between sheets of wax paper in an airtight container in the refrigerator for up to 10 days. Do not store at room temperature or freeze.

26 Crushed Vanilla Wafers
1/4 Cup Bourbon
1 Cup Sifted Powdered Sugar
1 Cup Finely Chopped, Toasted Pecans
3 Tbls. Unsweetened Cocoa Powder
2 Tbls. Light Corn Syrup

Sifted Powdered Sugar or Unsweetened Cocoa Powder

tip
Use a high grade bourbon; we tested with Jack Daniels Black Label.

Caution
Do not finely crush the wafers; the candy will turn mushy.

tip
These are the perfect dessert, served at the end of a full coarse Holiday meal.

Variation
Substitute brandy or rum for the bourbon.

✓
Favorite

The only complaint received about this recipe is - -
"I can't stop eating it!"

6 (3.3 oz.) Bags Natural
    Flavor Microwave Popcorn
3 Cups Packed Brown Sugar
2 1/4 Cups Light Corn Syrup
1 1/2 Cups Soft Butter
    (No Substitutions)
1/2 Tsp. Salt
1 1/2 Tsp. Baking Soda
5 x 9 Inch Treat Bags w/Ties
    (Optional)

tip

Do NOT use a heavy weight dark coated saucepan for cooking caramel mixture. It prevents the syrup from reaching the proper cooking temperature while boiling, and will result in overly chewy caramel corn.

1. Preheat oven to 250°. Microwave each popcorn bag on HIGH 2 minutes 40 seconds. Pour popped corn into a large oven roasting pan or large aluminum foil roasting pan. Pick out seeds and discard.

2. Combine sugar, syrup, butter and salt in a medium sized heavy saucepan over medium high heat. Stir continuously with a wooden spoon, until butter is melted and sugar is dissolved. If sugar crystals are present in sides of pan, wipe down with a damp paper towel. Bring mixture to a full boil.

3. Boil mixture over medium heat for 5 minutes, stirring constantly. Remove from heat and add soda. Stir well.

4. Pour caramel mixture evenly over popped corn. Using 2 large forks, toss popcorn with caramel mixture until evenly coated. Bake for 1 hour, stirring every 15 minutes. Remove from oven. Cool 20 minutes in the pan, then break up into bite sized pieces. Cool completely.

5. Store in an airtight container, or in treat bags with ties at room temperature for up to 3 weeks. Do not refrigerate or freeze.

This delightful concoction will get gobbled up
at your next group gathering!

1. Microwave the popcorn bags 2 minutes 40 seconds each.
Pour hot popcorn into a large wax paper lined roasting pan.
Let cool, and pick out seeds to discard.

2. Combine the popcorn, cereal puffs, corn chips, peanuts and
pretzels. Mix well.

3. Break almond bark into pieces and place in a medium sized
microwave safe bowl. Microwave on HIGH 90 seconds. Stir
well. Microwave on HIGH 60 more seconds. Stir again.
Continue to microwave in 15 second intervals, until smooth.
Let cool 3 minutes.

4. Drizzle melted coating over the popcorn mixture and stir
to coat all pieces. Let cool and set (about 1 hour).

5. Break mixture into pieces and transfer to an airtight
container or treat bags with ties. Store at room temperature
for up to 3 weeks. Do not refrigerate or freeze.

2 (3.3 oz.) Bags Natural Flavor
    Microwave Popcorn
4 Cups Corn Cereal Puffs
1 (10 oz.) Bag Corn Chips
2 Cups Dry Roasted or Cocktail
    Peanuts
2 Cups Thin Pretzel Sticks
1 1/2 Pounds Vanilla Flavored
    Almond Bark Coating
5 x 9 Inch Treat Bags w/Ties
    (Optional)

tip

*For testing purposes, we used 2 cups
each Kix and Corn Pops Brand Cereals,
and Fritos Brand Corn Chips.*

tip

*To evenly coat the popcorn, drizzle warm
almond bark over entire mixture with a
large spoon, then toss with 2 oversized
salad forks until well mixed.*

✓
Favorite

*Chocolate coated popcorn is enhanced
with marshmallows, nuts and coated chocolate candy pieces.*

3 (3.3 oz.) Bags Natural
   Flavored Microwave
   Popcorn
5 oz. Unsweetened Baking
   Chocolate
3/4 Cup Light Corn Syrup
3 Cups Sugar
1 1/2 Cups Water
1 Cup Miniature Candy Coated
   Chocolate Baking Pieces
1 Cup Cocktail or Dry Roasted
   Peanuts
2 Cups Miniature
   Marshmallows

5 x 9 Inch Treat Bags w/Ties
   (Optional)

1. Preheat oven to 200˚. Grease a large oven roasting or aluminum pan with cooking spray and set aside. Microwave each popcorn bag on HIGH 2 minutes 40 seconds. Pour popped corn into prepared pan.   Pick out seeds and discard. Place popcorn in oven to keep warm.

2. In a heavy 3 quart saucepan, melt chocolate and corn syrup over low heat, stirring occasionally. Stir in sugar and water. Cook and stir with a wooden spoon over medium heat, until mixture comes to a boil. Cook and occasionally stir to 250˚ (firm ball stage).

3. Pour hot mixture over warm popcorn, and quickly stir until evenly coated. Immediately add chocolate baking pieces, peanuts and marshmallows. Stir until well combined. Cool completely (about 1 hour).

4. Break mixture into pieces, and transfer to a foil covered container or treat bags with ties. Store at room temperature for up to 2 weeks. Do not refrigerate or freeze.

tip
For test purposes, we used M&M's Brand Miniature Candy Coated Baking Pieces, and Orville Redenbacher's Brand Light Natural Microwave Popcorn.

tip
Perform the candy thermometer test on page 246 to determine the proper cooking temperature at your altitude.

Variation
For more candy taste in the mixture, double the amounts of baking pieces, peanuts and marshmallows.

Peanut butter combines with sunflower seeds and roasted peanuts to give these festively wrapped bars a delightful flavor.

1. Preheat oven to 275˚. Line 2 (9 x 13 inch), or a (12 x 18 inch) baking pans with foil, leaving a 2-inch overhang on 2 sides. Grease with butter and set aside. Microwave each popcorn bag on HIGH 2 minutes 40 seconds. Pour popped corn into extra large mixing bowl. Pick out seeds and discard.

2. Combine corn syrup, honey, butter and sugar in a heavy 2 quart saucepan. Stir constantly with a wooden spoon, and cook over medium high heat, until mixture comes to a boil. Boil for 4 minutes, stirring occasionally. Remove from heat and stir in peanut butter and vanilla. Add nuts and kernels, and mix well. Pour mixture evenly over popcorn. Using 2 large forks, toss until evenly coated.

3. Transfer popcorn mixture to prepared pans. Use a spatula to compress into corners of pan. Bake 35 minutes. Remove to wire racks and cool completely.

4. When completely cool, remove popcorn from pan using foil edges to lift. Transfer to a flat cutting surface. Remove foil and use a cleaver or heavy duty knife to cut into desired sized sticks (we cut into (36) 6 inch by 1 inch sticks). Store popcorn in an airtight container, or wrapped in cellophane w/ ties at room temperature for up to 3 weeks. Do not refrigerate or freeze.

2 (3.3 oz.) Bags Natural Flavor Microwave Popcorn
3/4 Cup Light Corn Syrup
1/2 Cup Honey
1/3 Cup Soft Butter
1 1/4 Cups Sugar
2/3 Cup Creamy Peanut Butter
1 Tsp. Vanilla
1 Cup Dry Roasted Sunflower Kernels
1 Cup Cocktail or Dry Roasted Peanuts
Colored Cellophane w/ Ties (Optional)

tip

To measure peanut butter, pour 1 cup water into a 2 cup sized measuring cup. Then, add peanut butter until the water line reaches 1 2/3 cup. Drain the water and add the peanut butter to the recipe.

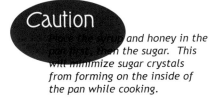

Caution

Place the syrup and honey in the pan first, then the sugar. This will minimize sugar crystals from forming on the inside of the pan while cooking.

Mountain City Moosey Bars

Sweet n' Salty

48 Coated Bar Cookies

√
Favorite

Here's our no-bake version of the popular
"s'mores" confection.

1 Cup Crunchy Peanut Butter
2 Cups Miniature
   Marshmallows
96 Graham Cracker "Sticks"
   (About 7 oz.)
16 oz. Milk Chocolate

tip

For test purposes, we used Nabisco Brand Honey Maid Cinnamon Sticks, and Hershey's Brand Milk Chocolate Bars.

tip

To measure peanut butter, pour 1 cup water into a 2 cup sized measuring cup. Then, add peanut butter until the water line reaches the 2 cups line. Drain the water.

1. Line baking sheets with wax paper. Spread a scant teaspoonful peanut butter on the flat side of the graham sticks. Place 3 miniature marshmallows in a line on top of the peanut butter. Top with another graham stick, peanut butter side down, and press together to form a sandwich (see photo).

2. Melt chocolate in a 1 quart oven proof saucepan using the oven method described on page 245. Dip each sandwich cookie into the melted chocolate. Shake off any excess, and place on prepared baking sheets to set (about 2 hours).

3. Do NOT cover chocolate until it is completely set. Store between sheets of wax paper in an airtight tin or foil covered container in a cool, dry, dark place (i.e. kitchen cabinet) for up to 3 weeks. Do not refrigerate or freeze.

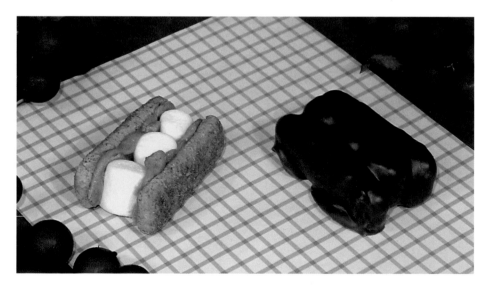

Variation

Substitute 1 Heaping Tsp. Marshmallow Cream instead of the marshmallows.

Low Sugar   Quick n' Easy   Favorite

A graham cracker never tasted so good!

1. Preheat oven to 350˚. Use a nut mill to finely chop pecans (see page 240). In a small mixing bowl, combine pecans, butter, brown sugar and vanilla. Mix well.

2. Using a spreader, spread 1 heaping teaspoon of the butter mixture on each cracker (be sure to cover cracker well).

3. Place 1 inch apart on ungreased baking sheets. Bake 10 minutes. Remove from oven, and leave on hot baking sheet to cool.

4. Store cookies between sheets of wax paper, in a foil covered container at room temperature for up to 10 days. Do not refrigerate or freeze.

1 Cup Finely Chopped Pecans
1/2 Cup Soft Butter
1/2 Cup Packed Brown Sugar
1/2 Tsp. Vanilla
15 Graham Crackers Broken
    Into 4 Sections Each

Here's a twist on the old fashioned "S'mores" treats.

2 Cups Coarsely Crushed Chocolate Graham Crackers
3/4 Cup Soft Butter
3/4 Cup Packed Brown Sugar
1 1/2 Cups Chopped Dry Roasted or Cocktail Peanuts (About 12 oz.)
4 Cups Miniature Marshmallows
1 Cup Candy-Coated Colored Milk Chocolate Pieces

tip

To chop peanuts and crush graham crackers, place separately in resealable plastic bags, and roll over several times with a rolling pin for desired sized pieces (see page 240).

tip

After you have added the chocolate pieces, gently press down on mixture with a spatula, to help set the chocolate into the marshmallows.

1. Heat oven to 350°. Grease a 9 x 13 inch glass baking dish with cooking spray. Spread graham cracker crumbs evenly in bottom of pan, making sure to cover entire area.

2. Melt the butter and brown sugar in a heavy 2-quart saucepan over medium heat. Stir constantly with a wooden spoon until mixture comes to a boil. Boil for 30 seconds. Drizzle mixture evenly over graham crackers, making sure to coat all the crumbs. Top evenly with crushed peanuts. Use a spatula, to compress mixture before baking.

3. Bake 10-12 minutes, or until bubbly. Remove from oven and immediately sprinkle evenly with marshmallows. Return to oven and continue baking until marshmallows begin to soften and puff (about 2-3 minutes). Watch carefully; you do not want marshmallows to brown on top. Remove from oven and sprinkle with candy pieces. Cool completely. Use a sharp edge to cut into 24 squares (6 rows by 4 rows).

4. Bars stay fresher if left uncut until served. Cover pan tightly with foil, and store at room temperature up to 3 days, or in the refrigerator up to 1 week. Do not freeze.

Variation

If chocolate graham crackers are unavailable, you may substitute the chocolate graham "sticks" sold in supermarkets next to the graham crackers.

√
Favorite

*Toasted macadamia nuts and bittersweet chocolate
nestled between graham cracker and caramel.*

1.   Preheat oven to 375˚. To coarsely chop the nuts, use a
chef's knife on a cutting board (see page 240). Line a
9 x 13 inch baking pan with parchment paper, leaving a
2 inch overhang on 2 sides.   Set aside.

2. Combine cracker crumbs, sugar and melted butter in a
medium sized mixing bowl, and stir until well combined. Using
fingers, firmly press crumb mixture evenly into prepared pan.

3. Melt the chocolate in a 1 quart oven proof saucepan
using the oven method described on page 245. Spread the
warm chocolate over the crumb base. Sprinkle the coconut
over the chocolate, and the nuts over the coconut.

4. Place the caramels and half n' half in a small sized
microwave safe bowl. Microwave on HIGH 2 minutes
15 seconds, stirring every 60 seconds. Drizzle warm caramel
mixture over nuts. Bake 20 minutes, or until golden brown.
Remove to wire rack to cool completely.

5. Remove cooled bars from pan using paper edges to lift.
Transfer to a flat cutting surface. Remove paper and use a
sharp edge to cut into 70 pieces (10 rows by 7 rows).
Store between sheets of wax paper in an airtight container.

6. Bars stay fresher if left uncut until served. Cover pan
tightly with foil and store at room temperature up to 3 days, or
in the refrigerator up to 10 days. Do not freeze.

2 Cups Graham Cracker
   Crumbs
1/4 Cup Sugar
1/3 Cup Melted Butter
12 oz. Bittersweet Baking
   Chocolate
1 1/2 Cups Packed Sweetened
   Flaked Coconut
3 Cups Coarsely Chopped
   Roasted Macadamia Nuts
14 oz. Caramels
2 Tbls. Half n' Half

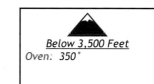

Below 3,500 Feet
Oven: 350˚

tip
*For test purposes, we used Ghiradelli
Brand Bittersweet Baking Chocolate.*

tip
*Half n' Half contributes to a
creamier caramel mixture.
Water or milk may be substituted.*

Variation
*Can substitute 2 cups bittersweet
flavored chocolate chips. Sprinkle
them on the crust underneath the
coconut and nuts, then bake as
directed.*

A butter toffee made with a saltine cracker - -
would you believe fantastic?

1 1/3 Cups Soft Butter, Divided
45 Saltine Cracker Squares
   (About 5 oz.)
1 Cup Packed Brown Sugar
14 oz. Can Sweetened
   Condensed Milk
1 2/3 Cups Semisweet
   Chocolate Chips
1 Cup Finely Chopped Walnuts
1/2 Cup Toffee Bits

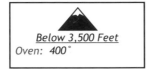

Below 3,500 Feet
Oven: 400°

tip

*If you don't have heavy duty foil
on hand, use 2 layers of regular
aluminum foil.*

tip

*For test purposes, we used Heath
Brand Toffee Chips.*

Caution

*Do not wait until candy is completely
cooled to remove from foil; the
candy will harden and make the foil
impossible to remove.*

1. Preheat oven to 425°. Line a 10 x 15 x 1 inch jelly roll pan with heavy duty foil, leaving a 2 inch overhang on 2 sides. Grease with butter and set aside. To chop nuts, use a nut mill.

2. Melt 1/3 Cup Butter in a 2 quart heavy saucepan over medium low heat until melted. Pour into prepared pan. Arrange crackers over butter, breaking crackers to fill empty spaces.

3. Melt the remaining 1 cup butter in the same saucepan. Add sugar. Bring to a boil over medium heat. Reduce heat to medium low, and cook, stirring occasionally, for 2 minutes. Remove from heat and stir in condensed milk. Drizzle evenly over crackers.

4. Bake 11-13 minutes, or until mixture is bubbly and slightly darkened. Remove from oven and cool for 1 minute. Immediately sprinkle with chocolate chips. Let stand 5 minutes, or until chips are shiny. Use a spreader to spread melted chips over mixture. Sprinkle with nuts and then toffee bits. Use a spatula to gently press nuts and toffee bits into the chocolate.

5. Let partially cool on a wire rack (about 20 minutes; see caution). While still warm, remove candy from pan using foil edges to lift. Transfer to a flat cutting surface. Remove foil and use a sharp edge to cut into 48 pieces (8 rows by 6 rows).

6. Do NOT cover chocolate until it is completely set. Store toffee pieces between sheets of wax paper in an airtight tin or foil covered container in a cool, dry, dark place (i.e. kitchen cabinet) for up to 2 weeks. Do not refrigerate or freeze.

Sweet n' Salty

Niwot's Nutty Clusters

Macadamia nuts transform these crispy white chocolatey treats into an expensive candy store favorite!

1. Line a baking sheet with parchment paper. Melt the white chocolate in a 2 quart oven proof saucepan using the oven method described on page 245. Meanwhile, chop the nuts with a chef's knife on a cutting board (see page 240). Set aside.

2. Stir the graham crackers and chopped nuts into the melted chocolate. Use 2 spoons; one to pick up the mixture and another to push mixture from the tip of the spoon onto the prepared baking sheet. Freeze clusters for 10 minutes to set. Remove from freezer and let sit at room temperature for 30 minutes.

3. Melt the dark chocolate in a 1 quart oven proof saucepan using the oven method described on page 245. Dip the tops of the room temperature clusters into the melted chocolate, allowing the excess to drip back into the pan. Return clusters to baking sheet and let set (about 2 hours).

4. Do NOT cover chocolate until it is completely set. Store between sheets of wax paper in an airtight tin or foil covered container in a cool, dry, dark place (i.e. kitchen cabinet) for up to 2 weeks. Do not refrigerate or freeze.

12 oz. White Baking Chocolate
3.5 oz. Graham Crackers,
    Broken in Small Pieces
    (About 8 Crackers)
1 Cup Coarsely Chopped
    Roasted and Salted
    Macadamia Nuts
8 oz. Dark Baking Chocolate

tip

For testing purposes, we used Nestle Brand Chocolatier Premium Baking Chocolates.

Caution

Do not dip COLD clusters into the chocolate; it will cause the chocolate to separate and appear "lumpy".

Variation

Try adding 1 cup miniature marshmallows to the mixture.

☑
Favorite

These turtle candies on a cracker
will become a favorite candy snack.

1 (14 oz.) Bag Caramels
2 Tbls. Half n' Half or Milk
1 1/2 Cups Coarsely Chopped
    Toasted Pecans
60 Butter-Flavored Crackers
8 oz. Milk or Dark Chocolate

tip

Using half n' half instead of
milk will create a creamier
caramel mixture.

tip

For test purposes, we used Ritz
Brand Crackers and Hershey's
Brand Chocolate Bars.

1. To toast pecans, arrange whole nuts in a single layer on a foil-lined baking sheet in a 350˚ oven for 8-10 minutes, stirring 2 or 3 times, until desired flavor is reached. Cool completely, then coarsely chop with a chef's knife on a cutting board (see page 240). Set aside.

2. Line a baking sheet with wax paper and set aside. Melt the chocolate in a 1 quart oven proof saucepan using the oven method described on page 245. Dip tops of crackers in chocolate to evenly coat, and set on prepared baking sheet to cool and set (about 1 hour).

3. Place caramels and half n' half in a small sized microwave safe bowl. Microwave on HIGH 2 minutes 15 seconds, stirring every 60 seconds until smooth. Add pecans, and stir until well combined.

4. Drop 1 heaping teaspoonful caramel mixture over each chocolate coated cracker. Let set (about 2 hours).

5. Store between sheets of wax paper in an airtight tin container, or foil covered container, at room temperature for up to 10 days. Do not refrigerate or freeze.

Caution

Make sure chocolate is hardened before
adding caramel mixture; otherwise, chocolate
may drizzle off the sides of the cracker.

Carson's Cranberry Crackles

A crispy cookie bar that's chock full of chocolate, cranberry and nuts.

1. Line a 9 x 9 inch pan with foil leaving a 2 inch overhang. Grease with butter and set aside.

2. Combine cereal, sunflower kernels, mini chocolate chips and cranberries a in medium sized mixing bowl. Set aside.

3. Break 12 oz. almond bark into pieces, and place in a medium sized microwave safe bowl. Microwave on HIGH 90 seconds. Stir well. Microwave on HIGH 60 more seconds. Stir again. If necessary, microwave in 15 second intervals until smooth. Let cool 3 minutes. Add butter and cereal mixture. Stir well. Spread mixture into prepared pan and compress with a spatula. Refrigerator 1 hour.

4. _Icing:_ Melt 6 oz. almond bark in a small microwave safe bowl (same instructions as above). Frost cooled bars and immediately sprinkle with mini chocolate chips. Let almond bark set, and then remove from pan using foil edges to lift. Transfer to a flat surface and cut with a sharp edge into 18 triangles.

5. Store between sheets of wax paper in an airtight container at room temperature for up to 1 week, or in the refrigerator up to 10 days. May freeze up to 4 months.

2 1/2 Cups Crispy Rice Cereal
1/2 Cup Dry Roasted Sunflower Kernels
1/4 Cup Miniature Semisweet Chocolate Chips
1/3 Cup Sweetened Dried Cranberries
1/2 Cup Melted Butter
12 oz. Vanilla Flavored Almond Bark Coating

Icing:
6 oz. Vanilla Flavored Almond Bark Coating
1/3 Cup Miniature Semisweet Chocolate Chips

tip
For test purposes, we used Rice Krispies Brand Cereal and Craisins Brand Dried Cranberries.

tip
To cut into 18 triangles, cut bars into 9 squares (3 rows by 3 rows). Then, diagonally cut each square in half.

Kids and adults alike,
will love this doubly delicious chocolate treat!

White Layer:
4 Tbls. Soft Butter
1 Tbls. Light Corn Syrup
6 oz. White Chocolate
2/3 Cup Crispy Rice Cereal
1/2 Cup Coarsely Chopped Dry
   Roasted or Cocktail
   Peanuts

Dark Layer:
4 Tbls. Soft Butter
2 Tbls. Light Corn Syrup
6 oz. Milk or Dark Chocolate
1 Cup Crispy Rice Cereal
1/2 Cup Coarsely Chopped Dry
   Roasted or Cocktail
   Peanuts

tip

To chop peanuts, place in a resealable plastic bag and roll over several times with a rolling pin for desired sized pieces (see page 240).

tip

For test purposes, we used Rice Krispies Brand Cereal.

Variation

Sunflower seeds or roasted soy nuts are delicious substitutions for the peanuts.

1. Line a 9-inch square pan with foil leaving a 2-inch overhang on 2 sides. Grease with butter and set aside.

2. To make the white chocolate layer, melt the butter over low heat in a 1 quart oven proof saucepan. Add corn syrup and white chocolate, and melt the chocolate mixture using the oven method described on page 245. Remove from oven, and stir in the cereal and peanuts until well combined. Spread evenly in bottom of the prepared pan. Freeze for 3 minutes, just until firm, then let sit at room temperature for 30 minutes.

3. To make the dark chocolate layer, melt the butter over low heat in a 1 quart oven proof saucepan. Add corn syrup and dark chocolate, and melt the chocolate mixture using the oven method described on page 245. Remove from oven, and stir in cereal and peanuts until well combined. Pour the dark chocolate mixture over the hardened white chocolate layer, and refrigerate until the top layer has hardened. At this point, you can cover candy tightly with foil, and refrigerate up to 1 week before cutting.

4. Remove candy from pan using foil edges to lift. Transfer to a flat cutting surface. Remove foil and use a sharp edge to cut into 20 pieces (5 rows by 4 rows).

5. Store between sheets of wax paper in an airtight container in the refrigerator for up to 1 week. Do not store at room temperature or freeze. Serve at room temperature.

✓
Favorite

This homemade candy resembles a popular candy bar.

1. Line 2 baking sheets with wax paper. Grease the paper with butter and set aside. Use a chef's knife on a cutting board to chop pecans. To toast the pecans, place chopped nuts in a single layer on a foil-lined baking sheet in a 350° oven for 6-8 minutes until crisp. Remove from oven and cool completely. Meanwhile, place caramels and half n' half in a medium sized microwave safe bowl. Microwave on HIGH 2 minutes 15 seconds, stirring every 60 seconds until smooth.

2. Add pecans and cereal to warm caramel mixture, and stir until well combined. Use 2 spoons, one to scoop up the mixture, and the other to drop mixture by rounded tablespoonfuls onto prepared baking sheets. Chill in the refrigerator for 15 minutes. Remove and let sit at room temperature for 30 minutes.

3. Melt chocolate in a 2 quart oven proof saucepan using the oven method described on page 245. Dip each candy into the chocolate, making sure to coat entire piece. Shake off excess chocolate, and place on wax paper sheets to set (about 2 hours).

4. Do NOT cover the candies until the chocolate has set and dried. Store between sheets of wax paper in an airtight tin, plastic craft container with lid, cardboard box with lid, or foil covered container. Keep in a cool, dry, dark place (i.e. closed kitchen cabinet), for up to 4 weeks. Do not refrigerate or freeze.

1 (14 oz.) Pkg. Caramels
3 Tbls. Half n' Half or Water
1 1/2 Cups Toasted Chopped
    Pecans
1 Cup Crispy Rice Cereal
24 oz. Milk Chocolate

tip

Using Half n' Half instead of water gives the caramel a creamier texture when melted.

tip

For testing purposes, we used Hershey Brand Milk Chocolate Bars, Kraft Brand Caramels, and Kellogg's Brand Rice Krispies Cereal.

Sweet n' Salty

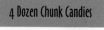

4 Dozen Chunk Candies

✓ Favorite   🕐 Quick n' Easy

This chunky sweet n' salty candy is loaded with nuts and crunch!

1 Cup Crispy Rice Cereal
1 Cup Puffed Corn Cereal
1 1/2 Cups Dry Roasted or Cocktail Peanuts
2/3 Cup Dry Roasted Sunflower Kernels
3 Cups Miniature Marshmallows
1 1/4 Cups Crunchy Peanut Butter
32 oz. Vanilla Flavored Almond Bark Coating

48 Mini Candy Cups

tip

To measure peanut butter, pour 3/4 cup water into a 2 cup sized measuring cup. then, add peanut butter until the water line reaches the 2 cup line. Drain the water.

tip

For test purposes, we used Kellogg's Brand Rice Krispies and Corn Pops Cereals.

1. Line a baking sheet with wax paper. In a large mixing bowl, combine the cereals, peanuts, sunflower kernels and marshmallows. Mix well. Place peanut butter in a microwave safe measuring cup, and microwave at 70% power for 1 minute 20 seconds. Stir until smooth, and pour over cereal mixture. Stir until well mixed.

2. Break almond bark into pieces, and place in a medium sized microwave safe glass bowl. Microwave on HIGH 90 seconds. Stir well. Microwave on HIGH 60 more seconds. Stir again. If necessary, microwave in 15 second intervals until smooth and creamy. Let cool 1 minute.

3. Add almond bark mixture to the cereal mixture, and stir until well combined. Let sit 3 minutes. Drop by tablespoonfuls onto prepared baking sheets. Let set (about 2 hours). Transfer to mini candy cups.

4. Store between sheets of wax paper in an airtight tin, loosely covered glass container or casserole dish, or foil covered container, in a cool place for up to 1 week, or in the refrigerator up to 3 weeks. Do not freeze.

Variation

For a touch of chocolate, add 1/2 cup miniature semisweet chocolate chips to the cereal mixture.

This combination of peanut butter, chocolate and crunchies is a winner!

1. Line a baking sheet with wax paper and set aside. Melt the peanut butter and butter in a 2 quart heavy saucepan over low heat. Meanwhile, in a large bowl, combine cereal, powdered sugar and peanuts.

2. Pour the melted peanut butter mixture over the cereal mixture. Stir until blended thoroughly. Use a small cookie scoop to form mixture into 1-inch balls, and place on prepared baking sheet. Freeze for 15 minutes to harden, then let sit at room temperature for 45 minutes before dipping into chocolate.

3. Melt the chocolate in a 2 quart oven proof saucepan using the oven method described on page 245. Dip each candy into chocolate, making sure to coat entire piece (see caution below). Shake off excess, and place on wax paper lined wire racks to cool and set (about 2 hours).

4. Do NOT cover the candies until the chocolate has set and dried. Store between sheets of wax paper in an airtight tin, plastic craft container with lid, cardboard box with lid, or foil covered container. Keep in a cool, dry, dark place (i.e. closed kitchen cabinet), for up to 3 weeks. Do not refrigerate or freeze.

2 1/2 Cups Creamy Peanut Butter
1/2 Cup Plus 2 Tbls. Soft Butter
3 Cups Crispy Rice Cereal
4 Cups Sifted Powdered Sugar
2/3 Cup Chopped Cocktail or Dry Roasted Peanuts
24 oz. Milk Chocolate

tip
For test purposes, we used Rice Krispies Brand Cereal and Hershey's Brand Milk Chocolate Bars.

Caution
Be sure the candies are at room temperature before dipping in warm chocolate; otherwise the chocolate will have a tendency to lump and tighten.

Quick n' Easy

*This pan cookie is piled high
with crispy ingredients!*

16 Full Size Graham Crackers
  (About 8 oz.)
2 1/2 Cups Miniature
  Marshmallows
1 Cup Soft Butter
1 Cup Packed Brown Sugar
1 Tsp. Cinnamon
1 Tsp. Vanilla
1 Cup Sliced Almonds
1 Cup Sweetened Flaked
  Coconut
1 Cup Chocolate Toffee Bits

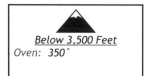

Below 3,500 Feet
Oven: 350˚

tip

*For test purposes,
we used Heath Brand
Chocolate Toffee Bits.*

1. Preheat oven to 375˚. Heavily grease a 10 x 15 x 1 inch jelly roll pan with butter, and set aside.

2. Arrange graham crackers in bottom of prepared pan. Break crackers to snugly fit in the pan. Sprinkle evenly with marshmallows.

3. Combine butter, brown sugar and cinnamon in a heavy 2 quart saucepan. Bring to a boil over medium heat. Boil, stirring constantly with a wooden spoon for 1 minute. Remove from heat, and stir in vanilla. Drizzle mixture evenly over graham crackers. Sprinkle evenly with almonds, coconut and toffee bits.

4. Bake 13-15 minutes, or until coconut is lightly toasted. Let cool in pan 10 minutes. Use a sharp knife to immediately cut into 48 pieces (8 rows by 6 rows). See Caution Below Left.

5. Store between sheets of wax paper in an airtight container at room temperature for up to 1 week, or in the refrigerator up to 2 weeks. Do not freeze.

Caution

Do not wait for candy to cool completely before cutting; it will stick to the pan, and become difficult to remove.

Quick n' Easy   Favorite ☑

Vail Valley Snowflake Crunchers

A breakfast cereal and coconut team up
for an incredible mouth watering morsel!

1. Preheat oven to 375°. Set aside ungreased baking sheets.

2. In a large mixing bowl, cream butter and shortening until well mixed (about 1 minute), scraping sides of bowl often. Add eggs and beat well. Combine flour, baking soda and salt. Add to mixture with milk, beating at medium speed, until well mixed. Add remaining ingredients on low speed, and mix just until combined.

3. Using a small cookie scoop, drop batter by rounded scoopfuls 2 inches apart onto baking sheets. Bake 12-14 minutes, or until lightly browned. Remove to wax paper lined wire racks to cool completely.

4. Store between sheets of wax paper in an airtight container at room temperature for up to 1 week, in the refrigerator up to 2 weeks, or in the freezer up to 4 months.

1/2 Cup Soft Butter
1/2 Cup Butter Flavored
    Shortening
2 Eggs
2 1/4 Cups Flour
1 Tsp. Baking Soda
1/2 Tsp. Salt
1/4 Cup Milk
2 Cups Corn Flakes Cereal
1 Cup Sweetened Flaked
    Coconut
1 Cup Packed Brown Sugar
1/2 Cup Dry Roasted Sunflower
    Kernels
1/2 Cup Roasted and Salted
    Soy Nuts
1/2 Cup Premier White Baking
    Chips

tip
For test purposes we used Kellogg's Brand Corn Flakes Cereal.

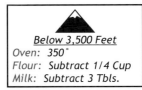

Below 3,500 Feet
Oven: 350°
Flour: Subtract 1/4 Cup
Milk: Subtract 3 Tbls.

tip

In cookie recipes, shortening contributes to a softer-textured and more cake like cookie.

Variation

For a breakfast cookie, add 1/2 cup dried cherries, cranberries or raisins to the batter.

☑
Favorite

*Here's a fruit filled breakfast bar
sure to please!*

4 Cups Granola Cereal
1/3 Cup Packed Brown Sugar
1/2 Cup Flour
1/2 Tsp. Salt
1/2 Cup Melted Butter
1 Cup Chopped Dried Apple
2/3 Cup Golden Raisins
14 oz. Can Sweetened
   Condensed Milk
1 Cup Coarsely Chopped
   Walnuts or Pecans

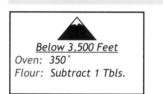

Below 3,500 Feet
Oven: 350˚
Flour: Subtract 1 Tbls.

tip

To chop walnuts, place in a resealable plastic bag and roll over several times with a rolling pin for desired sized pieces (see page 240).

1. Line a 9 x 13 inch baking pan with foil, leaving a 2-inch overhang on 2 sides. Grease heavily with butter (especially in the corners of the pan), and set aside. Preheat oven to 375˚.

2. Place granola in a resealable plastic bag and roll over several times with a rolling pin, until large chunks are crushed. In a large mixing bowl, combine granola, brown sugar, flour and salt. Stir well. Add butter, and stir until mixture is well combined. Use a spatula to compress cereal mixture evenly into the prepared pan. Bake for 10 minutes.

3. Remove from oven, and sprinkle dried apple and raisins over warm crust. Drizzle evenly with sweetened condensed milk. Sprinkle nuts on top, and compress with a spatula.

4. Bake 18-20 more minutes, or until top is light golden brown (do not overbake). Remove from oven and let cool 20 minutes. See Caution Below. Immediately remove bars from pan using foil edges to lift. Transfer to a flat cutting surface. Use a sharp edge to cut bars into 18 pieces (6 rows by 3 rows). Remove foil lining from bottoms of bars.

5. Wrap bars individually in plastic food wrap. Store between sheets of wax paper in an airtight container in the refrigerator up to 3 weeks. Do not store at room temperature or freeze.

Caution

Do not wait for mixture to cool completely before cutting bars. They will become difficult to remove from the foil lining in pan.

tip

For test purposes, we used Quaker Brand 100% Granola Cereal.

Conejos Cherry Crinkles

*Peanut butter and cherries combine to
create an unbelievably luscious no-bake treat!*

1. Line a baking sheet with wax paper and set aside. Use a chef's knife and cutting board to chop the nuts and cherries (see page 240). In a large mixing bowl, combine powdered sugar, peanut butter and butter. Beat until well mixed and creamy (about 1-2 minutes), scraping sides of bowl often. Stir in cereal, cherries, chocolate chips and pecans. Mix well.

2. Place coconut in a shallow bowl. Using a small cookie scoop, shape mixture into 1-inch balls. Roll in coconut, making sure to cover entire surface. Place close together on prepared baking sheet, and refrigerate 1 hour.

3. Store between sheets of wax paper in an airtight container in the refrigerator for up to 2 weeks. Do not store at room temperature or freeze.

1 1/4 Cups Powdered Sugar
1 1/4 Cups Creamy Peanut Butter
1/3 Cup Soft Butter
1 1/2 Cups Crispy Rice Cereal
1/2 Cup Maraschino Cherries, Drained, Dried and Chopped
1/2 Cup Miniature Semisweet Chocolate Chips
3/4 Cup Chopped Toasted Pecans
1 1/2 Cups Sweetened Flaked Coconut, Toasted

tip

Toasting the nuts and coconut enhances the flavor. To toast, place whole nuts and coconut together (but separated) on a foil-lined baking sheet in a 350° oven for 8-10 minutes, stirring 2 or 3 times, until desired flavor is reached. Cool completely.

Sweet n' Salty

☑ Favorite

This festive biscotti cookie is sweet and crisp; package in colored cellophane for a special gift.

1/2 Cup Soft Butter
3/4 Cup Sugar
3 Eggs
2 Tsp. Almond Extract
3 1/2 Cups Flour
2 Tsp. Baking Powder
2/3 Cup Chopped Candied
    Cherries
2/3 Cup Semisweet Chocolate
    Chips

8 oz. Dark Chocolate

Clear or Colored Cellophane
    (Not Plastic Food Wrap),
    Optional

Below 3,500 Feet
Oven: 350˚
Flour: Subtract 1/2 Cup

tip
Using a serrated knife to cut the cookies will result in a cleaner cut.

Caution
Do not over bake. Cookies will become more crisp as they cool.

Variation
Dip biscotti in white or milk chocolate instead of the dark chocolate.

1. Grease a large baking sheet pan with nonstick cooking spray and set aside. Preheat oven to 375˚. In a large mixing bowl, beat butter and sugar until smooth (about 1 minute), scraping sides of bowl often. Add eggs and almond extract, and beat until smooth (1 more minute). In a separate bowl, combine flour, baking powder, cherries and chocolate chips. Add to creamed mixture on low speed, and mix just until blended.

2. Using floured hands, shape dough into 2 (10 inch long by 3 inch wide) logs. Place 5 inches apart on prepared baking sheet (logs will spread during baking). Bake 23-25 minutes, or until set and light golden brown. Cool on hot baking sheet for 10 minutes. Remove logs to a cutting surface, and use a sharp knife to cut logs into 1/2 inch slices. Arrange slices cut side down, on warm baking sheet. Bake 8-10 minutes longer, or until bottoms begin to brown. Turn and bake 6-8 more minutes, or until lightly browned and crisp. Remove to wax paper lined wire racks to cool completely.

3. Melt the chocolate in a 1 quart oven proof saucepan using the oven method described on page 245. Dip the top inch of each cooled cookie into the melted chocolate. Return to wax paper lined rack to set (about 2 hours). For gift giving, wrap in clear or colored cellophane (not plastic wrap), and tie ends with fancy ribbon.

4. Do not store until chocolate has completely set up. Store in a container with a loose fitting lid (i.e. cookie jar or glass container with lid) at room temperature for up to 1 month. Do not refrigerate or freeze.

*These biscotti cookies are chock
full of cinnamon and nuts.*

1. Grease a large baking sheet or jelly roll pan with nonstick cooking spray, and set aside. Chop the walnuts using a nut mill (see page 240). Preheat oven to 375°.

2. In a large mixing bowl, beat butter and sugar until smooth (about 1 minute), scraping sides of bowl often. Add eggs and vanilla extract, and beat until smooth (1 more minute). In a separate bowl, combine flour, baking powder, salt, cinnamon, cinnamon chips and walnuts. Add to creamed mixture on low speed, and mix just until blended (dough will be stiff).

3. Using floured hands, shape dough into 3 (10 inch long by 2 inch wide) logs. Place 3 inches apart on prepared baking sheet (logs will spread during baking). Bake 22-24 minutes, or until set and light golden brown. Cool on hot baking sheet for 10 minutes. Remove logs to a cutting surface, and use a serrated sharp knife to cut logs into 1/2 inch slices.

4. Arrange slices cut side down, on warm baking sheet. Bake 7 minutes longer, or until bottoms begin to brown. Turn and bake 4-6 more minutes, or until lightly browned and crisp. Remove to wax paper lined wire racks to cool completely. Melt the chocolate in a 1 quart oven proof saucepan using the oven method described on page 245. Dip the top inch of each cooled cookie into the melted chocolate. Return to wax paper lined rack to set (about 2 hours).

5. Do not store until chocolate has completely set up. Store in a container with a loose fitting lid (i.e. cookie jar or glass container with lid) at room temperature for up to 1 month. Do not refrigerate or freeze.

1/2 Cup Soft Butter
1 Cup Sugar
2 Eggs
1 Tsp. Vanilla
2 1/2 Cups Flour
1 1/2 Tsp. Baking Powder
1/2 Tsp. Salt
1 Tsp. Cinnamon
1 Cup Cinnamon Chips
1 1/4 Cups Finely Chopped
    Walnuts

8 oz. White Chocolate

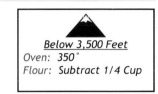
Below 3,500 Feet
Oven: 350°
Flour: Subtract 1/4 Cup

tip
For test purposes, we used Hershey's Brand Cinnamon Chips, sold in the baking section of your local supermarket.

Variation
For a special treat, add 1/2 cup miniature toffee baking bits to the batter.

Caution
Do not over bake; cookies will become more crisp as they cool.

☑
Favorite

This chocolate dipper cookie teams great with coffee;
it also keeps for a long time.

1 Cup Sugar
2/3 Cup Soft Butter
2 Cups Semisweet Chocolate
    Chips
3 Eggs
1 Tsp. Vanilla
2 3/4 Cups Flour
2 1/2 Tsp. Baking Powder
1/2 Tsp. Salt
1 Cup Finely Chopped
    Hazelnuts or Almonds

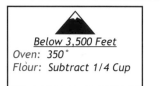

Below 3,500 Feet
Oven: 350˚
Flour: Subtract 1/4 Cup

tip

Use a mini chopper or chef's
knife on a cutting board to finely
chop nuts (see page 240).

Caution

Log will spread during baking; be
certain there is even space on all
sides of the logs before baking.
Do not over bake. Cookies will
become more crisp as they cool.

Variation

For a more elegant cookie, dip
the tip of cooled cookies in
melted chocolate.

1. Preheat oven to 350˚. Melt the chocolate chips in a 1 quart oven proof saucepan using the oven method described on page 245. In a large mixing bowl, combine sugar and butter. Beat at medium speed until well mixed. Add melted chocolate chips, eggs and vanilla. Continue beating until well mixed, scraping bowl often. Reduce speed to low, and add flour, baking powder and salt. Beat until well mixed. Stir in nuts by hand.

2. Divide dough in half. Shape each half into a 13-inch long by 2 1/2 inch wide log. Place the logs 3 inches apart on one large ungreased baking sheet or jelly roll pan. Bake 30 minutes, until set. Remove from oven and let cool on hot baking sheet for 15 minutes.

3. Reduce oven temperature to 300˚. Remove logs to a cutting surface, and cut into 1/2 inch slices with a serrated knife. Place on ungreased baking sheet, cut-side down. Bake 15 minutes. Turn slices; continue baking 15-17 minutes, or until dry and crisp. Remove from oven and cool completely on baking sheets.

4. Store in a container with a loose fitting lid (i.e. cookie jar or glass container with lid), at room temperature for up to 1 month. Do not refrigerate or freeze.

This chocolate chip and coffee flavored crisp cookie,
is perfect with a cup of steaming coffee or tea.

1. Grease a large baking sheet or jelly roll pan with nonstick cooking spray and set aside. Preheat oven to 350˚. Chop walnuts using a chef's knife and a cutting board (see page 240).

2. In a large mixing bowl, beat butter, sugars and coffee until smooth (about 1 minute), scraping sides of bowl often. Add eggs, and beat until smooth (1 more minute). In a separate bowl, combine flour, baking powder, cinnamon, salt, walnuts and chocolate chips. Add to creamed mixture on low speed, and mix just until blended (dough will be stiff).

3. Using floured hands, shape dough into 2 (10 inch long by 3 inch wide) logs. Place 5 inches apart on prepared baking sheet (logs will spread during baking). Bake 22-24 minutes, or until set and light golden brown. Cool on hot baking sheet for 10 minutes. Remove logs to a cutting surface, and use a sharp knife to cut into 1/2 inch slices.

4. Arrange slices cut side down, on warm baking sheet. Bake 6-8 minutes, or until bottoms begin to brown. Turn and bake 6-8 more minutes, or until lightly browned and crisp. Remove to wax paper lined wire racks to cool completely.

5. Store in a container with a loose fitting lid (i.e. cookie jar or glass container with lid) at room temperature for up to 1 month. Do not refrigerate or freeze.

1/2 Cup Soft Butter
1/2 Cup Packed Brown Sugar
1/2 Cup Sugar
1 Tbls. Instant Coffee Powder
2 Eggs
2 Cups Flour
1 1/2 Tsp. Baking Powder
1 Tsp. Cinnamon
1/4 Tsp. Salt
1 Cup Coarsely Chopped
    Walnuts
1 Cup Semisweet Chocolate
    Chips

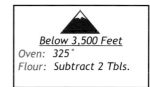

Below 3,500 Feet
Oven: 325˚
Flour: Subtract 2 Tbls.

tip
Logs will spread during baking; be certain there is even space on all sides of the logs on baking sheets.

Caution
Do not over bake. Cookies will become more crisp as they cool.

Variation
For a fancier cookie, dip the tops in your favorite flavor melted chocolate.

Don't Forget The Teacher And The Secretary . . .

Make a batch of "Mitzi's Mint Mallows"
on page 136.
Deliver with a decorated coffee mug full of instant
hot chocolate, tea or coffee packets, to the teachers
and secretaries in your life.
Attach a note telling them they are appreciated!

Mint Treasures

Popular flavors like mint and chocolate team up
to create timeless taste treats.
Many can be made ahead and frozen for
last minute get togethers.

Barrington Mints

✓
Favorite

These pretty mints are a party favorite - -
try them at your next special occasion!

8 oz. Soft Cream Cheese
6 Tbls. Soft Butter
3/4 Tsp. Pure Peppermint
      Extract (NOT Mint Extract)
2 Lbs. Sifted Powdered Sugar
1/2 Tsp. Vanilla
3 Drops Red Food Coloring

tip

*Sifting the powdered sugar
will result in a creamier mint.*

1. Melt the cream cheese with the butter in a heavy 3-quart saucepan over low heat, stirring constantly with a wooden spoon. Turn off the heat, leaving the pan on the burner, and stir in about 1 1/2 cups powdered sugar, food coloring and vanilla. Stir in the rest of the sugar until well blended.

2. Line a large baking sheet with wax paper. Push mint mixture into a pastry bag, icing syringe or squeeze bottle with a decorative tip. Create desired shapes for mints. Let set 1 hour.

3. Store between sheets of wax paper in an airtight container in the refrigerator for up to 1 month, or in the freezer up to 4 months. Do not store at room temperature.

Caution
*Peppermint extract is pretty
potent; measure it carefully.*

Variation
*Vary the food coloring and shape
of mint to fit the occasion.*

Sun Valley Swiss Mints

Quick n' Easy

This creamy chocolate mint melts in your mouth.

1. Line a 9 x 13 inch baking pan with mini candy cups. Set aside.

2. Break chocolate candy coating into pieces and place with unsweetened chocolate in a medium sized microwave safe bowl. Microwave on HIGH 90 seconds. Stir well. Microwave in additional 15 second increments, stirring after each, until creamy and smooth.

3. Pour condensed milk over chocolate, and add peppermint extract. Beat with an electric mixer just until blended. Use 2 ice tea spoons; one to pick up the mint mixture, and the other to push the candy from the tip of the spoon into the candy cups.

4. Cover pan tightly with foil, and store candies in the refrigerator for up to 2 weeks. Do not freeze or store at room temperature.

16 oz. Chocolate Flavored
   Candy Coating
2 oz. Unsweetened Baking
   Chocolate
14 oz. Can Sweetened
   Condensed Milk
1 Tsp. Pure Peppermint Extract
   (NOT Mint Extract)
Mini Candy Cups

tip

If mint mixture begins to set up, microwave on HIGH 15 seconds, then stir.

Manor House Truffles

4 Dozen Truffle Candies

✓ Favorite

These creamy minty truffles are double the chocolate mint inside and out!

1 1/2 Cups Sugar
3/4 Cup Soft Butter
3/4 Cup Evaporated Milk
2 Pkgs. (4.67 oz. each)
    Layered Chocolate Mint
    Candies (56 Mint Pieces)
10.5 oz. Marshmallow Cream
1 Tsp. Vanilla
16 oz. Milk Chocolate
1 Tsp. Pure Peppermint
    Extract

Drizzle:
3 oz. White Chocolate
3 Drops Green Food Coloring
48 Mini Candy Cups (Optional)

tip

For test purposes, we used Andes Brand Mint Candies.

tip

Use a plastic squeeze bottle to drizzle melted green chocolate in lines and squiggles over candies. If it becomes too thick, microwave it inside the bottle for 15 second intervals at 30% power.

1. Line baking sheets with wax paper and set aside.

2. Combine sugar, butter and milk in a 3 quart heavy saucepan over medium heat. Stir constantly until mixture comes to a boil. If sugar crystals are present, wipe down with a damp paper towel. Reduce heat to medium low, and cook and stir until a candy thermometer reads 236˚ (soft-ball stage). Remove from heat, and cool the mixture in pan for 3 minutes. Gently stir in mint candies until melted and smooth. Add marshmallow cream and vanilla, and mix well. Loosely cover, and refrigerate about 1 hour.

3. Use a small cookie scoop to form mixture into 1 1/4 inch disc shapes. Place on prepared baking sheets. Melt milk chocolate in a 2 quart oven proof saucepan using the oven method described on page 245. Gently add peppermint extract and stir until well mixed. Dip each candy piece into the melted chocolate, and shake off excess. Let set (about 2 hours).

4. Melt the white chocolate in a 1 quart oven proof saucepan using the oven method described on page 245. Add food coloring and stir until well combined. Drizzle in patterns over chocolates. Let set completely. Transfer to mini candy cups.

5. Do NOT cover chocolates until they have set completely. Transfer to an airtight tin or foil covered container in a cool, dry, dark place (i.e. closed kitchen cabinet) for up to 4 weeks. Do not refrigerate or freeze, as the humidity can cause chocolate coating to absorb moisture and separate.

Caution
Let mixture cool before adding mints. Otherwise, chocolate will burn.

2 Pounds

Quick n' Easy   Favorite

Marlene's Magic Mint Fudge

*This oh-so-easy mint fudge
is pure chocolate decadence!*

1. Line a 9-inch square pan with foil leaving a 2-inch overhang on 2 sides. Grease with butter and set aside.

2. Melt the candy bars together in a 2 quart oven proof saucepan using the oven method described on page 245. Remove from oven, and gently stir in the condensed milk, peppermint extract and vanilla until well blended. Spread into the prepared pan. Refrigerate uncovered until set (about 2 hours).

3. Remove fudge from pan using foil edges to lift. Transfer to a flat cutting surface. Remove foil, and using a sharp edge, cut into 81 pieces (9 rows by 9 rows).

4. Store between sheets of wax paper in an airtight container in the refrigerator up to 3 weeks. To freeze, cut large pieces (3 by 3 inch squares), wrap individually in plastic food wrap, and store in an airtight container in the freezer for up to 6 months. Do not store at room temperature.

8 oz. Dark Chocolate Candy Bars
16 oz. Milk Chocolate Candy Bars
14 oz. Can Sweetened Condensed Milk
1 Tsp. Pure Peppermint Extract (NOT Mint Extract)
1 Tsp. Vanilla

tip

To line a pan with foil without tearing it, invert the pan and shape the foil over the bottom. Lift the shaped foil off and fit it into the upright pan, pressing it gently into the corners (see page 238).

tip

For test purposes, we used Hershey's Brand Special Dark and Milk Chocolate Candy Bars.

Caution

Do not over stir; it will create a coarse fudge. Use a rubber spatula and gently fold ingredients just until combined.

Mitzi's Mint Mallows

2 Dozen Candies

Favorite   Quick n' Easy

Serve these chocolate coated marshmallows as an after dinner mint.

12 Large Marshmallows, Cut in Half
1/2 Tsp. Pure Peppermint Extract (NOT Mint Extract)
8 oz. Milk Chocolate
1/3 Cup Crushed Peppermint Candy Canes

tip

For test purposes, we used Hershey's Brand Milk Chocolate Bars, and Wilton's Brand Peppermint Crunch Sprinkles.

1. Line a baking sheet with wax paper. Cut marshmallows in half with a pair of kitchen shears, and set aside.

2. Melt the chocolate in a 1 quart oven proof saucepan using the oven method described on page 245. Gently stir in extract. Dip marshmallows in melted chocolate, shaking off excess. Set on prepared baking sheet, and immediately sprinkle with crushed peppermint. Let set (about 2 hours).

3. Do NOT cover chocolate until it has dried completely. Transfer to an airtight tin, or foil covered container in a cool, dry, dark place (i.e. closed kitchen cabinet) for up to 1 month. Do not refrigerator or freeze.

Favorite

Mint Treasures

Palmer Lake Minty Melts

These chocolate covered peppermint balls make perfect bite-sized desserts!

1. Line baking sheets with wax paper and set aside. To crush cookies, place in a heavy duty resealable plastic bag, and roll over several times with a rolling pin until finely crushed.

2. Combine cookie crumbs and nuts in a medium sized mixing bowl. Add butter and Peppermint Schnapps. Stir until well combined. Using a small cookie scoop, form candy into 1 inch balls, and place on prepared baking sheets. Refrigerate about 1 hour.

3. Melt the chocolate in a 1 quart oven proof saucepan using the oven method described on page 245. Dip each candy piece into the melted chocolate, and shake off excess. Let set (about 2 hours). Transfer to mini candy cups.

4. Do NOT cover chocolate until it has dried completely. Store between sheets of wax paper in an airtight tin, or foil covered container in a cool, dry, dark place (i.e. closed kitchen cabinet) for up to 3 weeks. Do not refrigerate or freeze, as humidity can cause the chocolate to absorb moisture and separate.

2 Cups Crushed Thin Chocolate Covered Mint Cookies (10 oz. Bag)
1 Cup Finely Chopped Toasted Walnuts
5 Tbls. Melted Butter
1/4 Cup Peppermint Schnapps Liqueur
12 oz. Milk Chocolate

Mini Candy Cups (Optional)

tip
To toast walnuts, place whole nuts in a single layer on a foil-lined baking sheet in a 350˚ oven for 8-10 minutes, stirring 2 or 3 times, until desired flavor is reached. Cool Completely. To finely chop the walnuts, use a nut mill (see page 240).

tip
For test purposes, we used Keebler Brand Grasshopper Cookies, and Hershey's Brand Milk Chocolate Bars.

Custer's Candy Cane Bon Bons

50 Bon Bons

☑ Favorite   🕐 Quick n' Easy

A chocolate peppermint candy so easy to make, and so delectable!

8 oz. Milk Chocolate
1 Cup Semisweet Chocolate
    Chips
20 Crushed Chocolate
    Sandwich Cookies (About
    2 Cups)
1/2 Cup Finely Crushed
    Peppermint Candy Canes
Mini Candy Cups

1. Line a baking sheet with 50 mini candy cups; set aside.

2. Melt the milk chocolate with the chocolate chips in a 2 quart oven proof saucepan, using the oven method described on page 245. Gently stir in crushed cookies and peppermint candy pieces. Stir until well combined.

3. Use 2 ice tea spoons; one to pick up the candy mixture, and the other to push candy from the tip of the spoon into the mini candy cups. Immediately sprinkle with additional peppermint candies. Let set (about 2 hours).

4. Store between sheets of wax paper in an airtight container at room temperature for up to 3 days, or in the refrigerator up to 2 weeks. Do not freeze. Serve at room temperature.

tip

To crush cookies, place in a resealable plastic bag and run over with a rolling pin for desired sized pieces (see page 240).

tip

For test purposes, we used Oreos Brand Chocolate Sandwich Cookies, and Wilton's Brand Sprinkles Peppermint Crunch.

Moffat's Mint Drizzles

Super quick, this cream cheese based cookie dough is baked and topped with a drizzled chocolate mint candy.

1. Preheat oven to 375°. Grease a 10 x 15 inch glass baking dish with nonstick cooking spray. Lightly dust with flour and set aside.

2. In a large mixing bowl, beat cream cheese, butter, sugar, food coloring and mint extract until blended, scraping sides of bowl often. Add flour, baking soda and milk, and beat until combined. Using fingers, pat dough evenly into prepared pan. Use a mini rolling pin to even out the dough to all edges in the pan. Bake 18-20 minutes, or until a toothpick inserted in the center, comes out clean.

3. Remove pan from oven, and immediately place unwrapped mint candies in rows (10 rows by 4 rows), on warm pan cookie. Let sit 5 minutes. Use a toothpick to swirl each individual chocolate mint candy on top of cookie. Immediately sprinkle peppermint candies on top. Cool Completely. Use a sharp edge to cut into rectangles (same shape as mint), so the mint candy lies on top of each cookie.

4. Store between sheets of wax paper in an airtight container in the refrigerator up to 10 days, or in the freezer up to 4 months. Do not store at room temperature.

8 oz. Soft Cream Cheese
3/4 Cup Soft Butter
1 1/4 Cups Powdered Sugar
6 Drops Green Food Coloring
1 Tsp. Pure Peppermint
    Extract
2 1/4 Cups Flour
1 Tsp. Baking Soda
2 Tbls. Milk
40 Layered Chocolate Mint
    Candies
1/2 Cup Crushed Peppermint
    Candies

Below 3,500 Feet
Oven: 350°
Flour: Subtract 1/4 Cup
Milk: Do Not Add Milk

tip

For test purposes, we used Starlight Brand Hard Peppermint Candies. To crush, place candies in a mini chopper and pulse several times until crushed. Store in a tightly sealed canning jar.

tip

For the chocolate mint, we used Andes Brand Mint Candies.

Variation

Roll the dough out to 1/4" thickness and use your favorite cookie cutter to create a mint cutout cookie. As soon as you remove the cookies from the oven, top them with the chocolate mint and crushed candies.

Caution

...not use a metal pan; ...will result in a dry cookie.

This shortbread cookie with a soft mint in the middle --
will become a snack favorite with kids of all ages!

1 Cup Buttered Flavored
   Shortening
8 oz. Soft Cream Cheese
3/4 Cup Sugar
1/2 Cup Packed Brown Sugar
1 Tsp. Vanilla
2 1/4 Cups Flour
54 Miniature Chocolate Coated
   Mint Cream Candies

Icing:
2 Cups Powdered Sugar
3 Tbls. Melted Butter
1 Tbls. or More Half n' Half
1/2 Tsp. Pure Peppermint
   Extract
2 Drops Red Food Coloring
Peppermint Sprinkles

Below 3,500 Feet
Oven: 325˚
Flour: Subtract 1/4 Cup

tip
For test purposes, we used Junior Mint Brand Mint Candies and Cake Mate Brand Peppermint Flavored Sugar Sprinkles.

tip
Shortening contributes to a softer-textured and more cake like cookie.

1. Preheat oven to 350˚. Grease baking sheets with nonstick cooking spray and set aside. In a large mixing bowl, combine shortening, cream cheese, sugars and vanilla. Beat until creamy, scraping sides of bowl often (about 1-2 minutes). Add flour to mixture at low speed, just until blended.

2. Using a small spoon, form a 3/4 inch dough ball around each individual mint (thus; mint in the middle). Be sure to cover all sides of the mint with dough. Place on prepared baking sheets 2 inches apart. Bake 10-12 minutes, or until lightly browned. Let cookies sit on hot baking sheet for 2 minutes, then remove and cool completely on wax paper lined wire racks.

3. Icing: Combine all icing ingredients except sprinkles in a small bowl. Beat until smooth. Add more half n' half if necessary. Frost the top half of each cookie, and immediately add sprinkles on top. Let set (about 1 hour).

4. Store between sheets of wax paper in an airtight container at room temperature for up to 1 week, or in the refrigerator up to 10 days. Unfrosted cookies keep 4 months in your freezer. Thaw at room temperature, then frost and decorate.

Caution
Mint filling will escape from the cookie while baking if you do not completely cover the mint with dough.

Quick n' Easy   Favorite

Mint Treasures

Missoula Mint Rounds

Try all three sugars; red, green and white, to add a special
"minty" touch to your cookie tray.

1. Preheat oven to 375˚. In a small bowl, combine the flour, baking powder and salt. Set aside.

2. In a large mixing bowl, combine sugar and oil. Add eggs, one at a time, beating well after each addition. Blend in vanilla extract.

3. Gradually beat in flour mixture at medium speed, scraping the side of the bowl often. Stir in mint chocolate chips. Using a small cookie scoop (see page 239), shape dough into balls, and roll in colored or white sugar. Place 2 inches apart on un-greased baking sheets.

4. Bake 8-9 minutes, or until set. Remove from oven and let stand on hot cookie sheets for 2 more minutes. Remove to wax paper lined wire racks and cool completely.

5. Store cookies between sheets of wax paper in an airtight container at room temperature for up to 1 week, in the refrigerator up to 10 days, or in the freezer up to 4 months.

2 1/2 Cups Flour
1 1/4 Tsp. Baking Powder
3/4 Tsp. Salt
1 Cup Sugar
3/4 Cup Vegetable Oil
2 Eggs
1 Tsp. Vanilla
1 Cup Mint Flavored Chocolate
    Chips
Assorted Colored and White
    Sugars

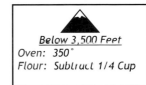

Below 3,500 Feet
Oven: 350˚
Flour: Subtract 1/4 Cup

tip

If mint chips are not available, place 1 cup semisweet chocolate chips and 1/2 tsp. pure peppermint extract in a resealable plastic bag; seal and toss to coat. Let stand at room temperature for 24-48 hours.

Pinehurst Peppermint Sticks

*A cup of coffee or cocoa and a peppermint biscotti - -
can you think of a better way to kick off a neighborhood get together?*

3/4 Cup Soft Butter
3/4 Cup Sugar
3 Eggs
2 Tsp. Pure Peppermint Extract
   (NOT Mint Extract)
3 1/2 Cups Flour
1 Tsp. Baking Powder
1/2 Tsp. Salt
1 Cup Peppermint Flavored
   Baking Chips

<u>Coating:</u>
16 oz. Milk Chocolate
1/2 Cup Peppermint Sprinkles

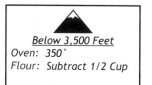

Below 3,500 Feet
Oven: 350°
Flour: Subtract 1/2 Cup

tip

For test purposes, we used Andes Brand Peppermint Crunch Baking Pieces, Hershey's Milk Chocolate Candy Bars, and Cake Mate Brand Peppermint Flavored Sugar.

tip

Remove biscotti from oven as soon as they are firm and light golden brown. They will become crisper as they cool.

1. Preheat oven to 375°. In a large mixing bowl, cream butter and sugar, scraping sides of bowl often, until well combined. Add eggs and extract, and beat well (about 1-2 minutes). Combine flour, baking powder, salt and peppermint chips in a small bowl, and stir to combine. Add flour mixture to dough, and stir just until combined (dough will be stiff).

2. Divide dough in half, and shape each half into a 12 inch by 3 inch rectangular log. Place on ungreased baking sheets and bake 20-22 minutes, or until golden brown. Remove from oven and leave on hot baking sheet for 10 minutes.

3. Immediately transfer to a cutting board, and use a sharp knife to cut into 1/2 inch slices. Return slices to baking sheets and bake 14-16 minutes, or until firm and golden brown. Remove to wax paper lined wire racks to cool completely.

4. Melt the chocolate in a 1 quart oven proof saucepan using the oven method described on page 245. Dip the top inch of each biscotti cookie in melted chocolate. Shake off excess, and place on wax paper lined surface to set up for 2 minutes. Immediately sprinkle with peppermint sprinkles on one side, and let set (about 2 hours).

5. Do NOT cover chocolate until it has dried completely. Store between sheets of wax paper in a container with a loose fitting lid (i.e. cookie jar or glass casserole container with lid) at room temperature for up to 1 month. Do not refrigerate or freeze.

Monty's Mint Meltaways

These chocolate mint pillow cookies have a double mint coating.

1. Preheat oven to 400˚. Spray baking sheets with nonstick cooking spray and set aside. Combine all cookie ingredients except flour, in a large mixing bowl. Beat at medium speed for 1 minute, scraping bowl often, until well mixed. Gradually add flour, and beat on low speed, just until combined.

2. Using a small cookie scoop (see page 239), drop dough by rounded scoopfuls 2 inches apart onto prepared baking sheets. Bake 8-10 minutes, or until cookie springs back when touched lightly in center. Cool completely on wax paper lined wire racks.

3. <u>Icing:</u> Combine all ingredients except crushed peppermint in a small bowl. Beat at medium speed until creamy. Spread about 1 tablespoon icing on each cookie, and immediately sprinkle with peppermint candy. Place frosted cookies inside a 9 x 13 inch baking pan lined with wax paper. Immediately cover the pan tightly with foil. Let set (about 2 hours). When you remove the foil, the mints will have "melted" away!

4. Store between sheets of wax paper in an airtight container at room temperature for up to 1 week, or in the refrigerator up to 10 days. Unfrosted cookies keep 4 months in your freezer. Thaw at room temperature, then frost and decorate.

2 Cups Sugar
1 Cup Unsweetened Cocoa
    Powder
1 Cup Soft Butter
1 Cup Buttermilk
1 Cup Water
2 Eggs
2 Tsp. Baking Soda
1 Tsp. Baking Powder
2 Tsp Vanilla
1 Tsp. Salt
4 1/2 Cups Flour

Icing:
3/4 Cup Melted Butter
4 Cups Sifted Powdered Sugar
1/4 Cup or More Milk
    as Needed
2 Tsp. Vanilla
1 Tsp. Pure Peppermint Extract
    (NOT Mint Extract)
4 Drops Red Food Coloring
1/2 Cup Crushed Peppermint
    Candy Canes

Caution
Do not over beat the batter; it will result in a tough cookie.

Below 3,500 Feet
Oven: 375˚
Flour: Subtract 1/2 Cup
Water: Subtract 1/3 Cup

tip
For test purposes, we used Wilton's Brand Peppermint Crunch Sprinkles.

Windsor's Peppermint Nougats

√
Favorite

This combination of cookie and candy coating, creates a bite sized confection perfect for munching!

1 1/2 Cups Vanilla Wafer Crumbs
1 Cup Crushed Peppermint Candies
1/2 Cup Melted Butter
1 Cup Sliced Almonds

Icing:
6 oz. Vanilla Flavored Almond Bark Coating
3 Drops Red Food Coloring

tip

For test purposes, we used Starlight Brand Hard Peppermint Candies. To crush peppermint candies, place in a mini chopper and pulse several times until crushed. Store in a tightly sealed canning jar.

1. Preheat oven to 350˚. Place vanilla wafers in a resealable plastic bag, and roll over several times with a rolling pin until coarse crumbs form. Line a 9 x 13 inch baking pan with foil, and grease with nonstick cooking spray. Set aside.

2. Combine crumbs and crushed peppermint candies in a medium sized mixing bowl. Stir to combine. Add butter and nuts, and stir until well combined. Use fingers to spread mixture evenly into prepared pan. Then, use a spatula to compress mixture. Bake 18 minutes, or until very light golden brown. Remove to wire rack to cool completely.

3. Break up almond bark pieces, and place in a small microwave safe bowl. Microwave on HIGH 60 seconds. Stir well. Microwave in 15 second increments, stirring after each, until smooth and creamy. Add food coloring and stir well.

4. Use a spoon to immediately drizzle almond bark mixture in designs over cooled candy. Let set (about 1 hour)

5. When set, use a sharp edge to cut into 45 bite-sized chunks (9 rows by 5 rows).

6. Store between sheets of wax paper in an airtight container at room temperature for up to 1 week, in the refrigerator up to 3 weeks. Do not freeze.

Meeker's Mint Macaroons

These light as a feather minty cookies have a surprise ingredient - - breakfast cereal!

1. Preheat oven to 350°. Spray baking sheets with nonstick cooking spray and set aside.

2. In a medium sized mixing bowl, beat egg whites until foamy. Gradually add sugar, beating until stiff and glossy (about 2-3 minutes).

3. Add cereal, crushed peppermint and vanilla, and stir until well blended. Using a small cookie scoop (see page 239), drop dough by rounded scoopfuls, 2 inches apart onto prepared baking sheets.

4. Bake 12 minutes, or until firm to the touch. Remove from oven and immediately transfer to wax paper lined wire racks to cool completely. Lightly dust cookies with sifted powdered sugar.

5. Store between layers of wax paper in an airtight container at room temperature for up to 1 week. Do not refrigerate or freeze.

2 Egg Whites at Room Temperature
1 Cup Sugar
2 Cups Lightly Toasted Rice Cereal
1/2 Cup Crushed Peppermint Candy Canes
1 Tsp. Vanilla
Sifted Powdered Sugar

tip
Remove eggs from the refrigerator 20-30 minutes before baking. Remember, eggs separate more easily when they are COLD.

tip
For test purposes we used Kellogg's Brand Special K Cereal and Wilton's Brand Sprinkles Peppermint Crunch.

Variation
For a touch of chocolate, add 1/2 cup miniature semisweet chocolate chips.

Palisade Peppermint Tidbits

Mint Treasures

√ Favorite   Low Sugar

*Enjoy lots of mint chocolate in these bite-sized,
light as a feather, peppermint glazed cakes.*

1/2 Cup Soft Butter
4 oz. Soft Cream Cheese
3/4 Cup Sugar
2 Eggs
1 Tsp. Vanilla
1 Cup Flour
1 Tsp. Baking Powder
1 Cup Mint Flavored Chocolate
    Chips
5 Drops Green Food Color

Mint Glaze:
1 1/4 Cups Mint Flavored
    Chocolate Chips
3 Tbls. Butter Flavored
    Shortening (No
    Substitutions)

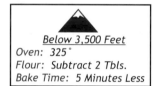

Below 3,500 Feet
Oven: 325˚
Flour: Subtract 2 Tbls.
Bake Time: 5 Minutes Less

tip

*If mint chips are not available, place
2 1/4 cups semisweet chocolate chips
and 1 teaspoon pure peppermint
extract in a resealable plastic bag.
Seal and toss to coat. Let stand at
room temperature for 24-48 hours.*

Caution
*Do not use a metal
baking pan for this
recipe, it will result
in a dry brownie.*

1. Preheat oven to 350˚. Grease a 9 x 13 inch baking dish (glass only) and dust with flour. Line a baking sheet with wax paper. Set aside.

2. In a large mixing bowl, cream butter, cream cheese and sugar until fluffy (about 1 minute). Scrape sides of bowl often. Add eggs and vanilla and beat well. Combine flour and baking powder and stir into mixture. Add mint chips and food coloring, and stir until well combined.

3. Spread batter into prepared pan, and bake 25-30 minutes until toothpick inserted in center comes out clean. Remove to wire rack to cool completely.

4. Mint Glaze: Combine chips and shortening in a medium sized microwave safe measuring cup. Microwave at 80% power for 60 seconds. Stir. Microwave at 80% power in 15 second increments, until mixture is smooth and runny. Using a sharp edge, cut brownies into 40 pieces (8 rows by 5 rows). Place pieces 2 inches apart on prepared baking sheet. Use an ice tea spoon, to drizzle glaze over brownie pieces, letting it drizzle down sides (see photo).

5. Brownies stay fresher if left uncut until served. Cover pan tightly with foil, until ready to serve. At serving time, cut brownies and glaze as instructed above. May store loosely covered at room temperature for up to 8 hours. We do not recommend refrigerating or freezing bars.

Maxine's Mint Chip Divinity

✓
Favorite

*This pink peppermint chocolate swirl divinity is simply heaven on earth!
It's best to wait for a dry weather day, as humidity can affect the texture.*

1. Line a baking sheet with wax paper and set aside.

2. In a large mixing bowl, beat the egg whites and salt. When soft peaks form, set aside. Combine the sugar, water and corn syrup in a 2 quart heavy saucepan. Cook over medium heat, and stir with a wooden spoon, until sugar is completely dissolved and the mixture comes to a boil. If sugar crystals are present, wipe down sides of pan with a damp paper towel.

3. Increase heat to medium high, and cook, without stirring, until the mixture reaches 260° (hard ball stage; about 7-8 minutes). Immediately remove pan from heat. Re-beat the egg whites for a few seconds to blend any separation. With the beater running at high speed, slowly and carefully pour the hot syrup into the egg whites in a thin, steady stream. Beat until the divinity begins to lose its sheen (about 30 seconds). Stop the mixer, scrape sides of bowl, add vanilla, peppermint extract and food color, and continue to beat, until mixture holds its shape when dropped from a spoon (about 8 minutes).

4. Using a rubber spatula, gently fold in candies first, and then chocolate chips. Stir just until chips are incorporated. Immediately drop mixture by tablespoonfuls onto prepared baking sheet. Let set (about 20 minutes).

5. Store between sheets of wax paper in an airtight container, in a cool, dry place at room temperature for up to 10 days. Do not refrigerate or freeze.

2 Egg Whites at Room
    Temperature
1/2 Tsp. Salt
2 1/2 Cups Sugar
2/3 Cup Water
1/2 Cup Light Corn Syrup
1 Tsp. Vanilla
1/2 Tsp. Pure Peppermint
    Extract
7 Drops Red Food Coloring
1/2 Cup Crushed Peppermint
    Candies
1/2 Cup Semisweet Chocolate
    Chips

tip

Perform the candy thermometer test on page 246 to determine the proper cooking temperature at your altitude.

tip

Remove eggs from the refrigerator 20-30 minutes before candy making. Remember, eggs separate more easily when they are COLD.

Caution

Do not over beat; candy will become grainy. We recommend you use a minute timer with this recipe (see page 241).

Allenspark Marbled Mint Bark

72 Mint Candies

☑ Favorite ⏰ Quick n' Easy

These chocolate layered candies are sweet and creamy, with just the right amount of peppermint crunch.

6 oz. Chocolate Flavored
   Candy Coating
6 oz. Milk Chocolate
6 oz. Vanilla Flavored Almond
   Bark Coating
6 oz. White Chocolate
1/4 Cup Crushed Peppermint
   Candy

tip

For test purposes, we used Hershey's Brand Milk Chocolate Bars, Baker's Brand Premium White Chocolate Baking Squares, and Wilton Brand Peppermint Crunch Sprinkles.

1. Line a 9 x 13 inch pan with foil leaving a 2-inch overhang on 2 sides. Grease with butter and set aside.

2. Break chocolate candy coating and milk chocolate into pieces, and place together in a medium sized microwave safe bowl. Microwave at 60% power for 2 1/2 minutes, stirring every 60 seconds. Stir until smooth, and spread evenly in prepared pan. Let stand for 5 minutes.

3. Break almond bark and white chocolate into pieces and place in a medium sized microwave safe bowl. Microwave at 60% power for 2 1/2 minutes, stirring every 60 seconds. Drizzle white chocolate mixture evenly over chocolate mixture. Use a small rubber spatula, to quickly swirl white mixture into chocolate mixture. Immediately sprinkle with peppermint crunch candy.

4. Chill 30 minutes or until set. Remove candy from pan using foil edges to lift. Transfer to a flat cutting surface. Remove foil and use a cleaver or heavy duty knife to cut into 72 pieces (9 rows by 8 rows). Do not cover candy until it has dried completely.

5. Store between sheets of wax paper in an airtight tin or foil covered container in a cool, dry, dark place (i.e. closed kitchen cabinet) for up to 4 weeks. Do not refrigerate or freeze.

Barney's Buttermint Bark

Quick n' Easy   Favorite ✓

*With butter mints hidden in the middle,
this simple chocolate candy is amazing!*

1. Line a baking sheet with mini candy cups and set aside. Melt the chocolate in a 2 quart oven proof saucepan using the oven method described on page 245.

2. Remove chocolate from oven, and very gently stir in chopped mints and extract just until combined.

3. Use 2 ice tea spoons, one to pick up the candy, and the other to push candy from the tip of the spoon into the mini candy cups. Let set (about 2 hours).

4. Do NOT cover chocolate until it has dried completely. Layer between sheets of wax paper in an airtight tin or foil covered container in a cool, dry, dark place (i.e. closed kitchen cabinet) for up to 4 weeks. Do not refrigerate or freeze.

12 oz. Milk Chocolate
6 oz. Box Butter Mints,
   Chopped in Half
      (Not Pastel Mints)
1/2 Tsp. Pure Peppermint
   Extract (NOT Mint Extract)

Mini Candy Cups

tip

"Butter" Mints are sold in a box found in the candy section of supermarkets or drug stores. Use a chef's knife and a cutting board to chop mints in half (see page 240).

Caution
*Do not over stir the chocolate;
it will lose it's smooth texture.*

√
Favorite

*These layered brownie cookies
contain a candy bar in the middle!*

Oat Base:
1 Cup Packed Brown Sugar
2/3 Cup Soft Butter
1/4 Cup Light Corn Syrup
1/2 Cup Creamy Peanut Butter
1 Tsp. Vanilla
1 Egg
1 1/2 Cups Flour
2 1/4 Cups Quick Cooking
   Rolled Oats

Topping:
1 1/2 Cups Semisweet
   Chocolate Chips
3/4 Cup Butterscotch Flavored
   Chips
1/2 Cup Smooth Peanut Butter
14 oz. Can Sweetened
   Condensed Milk
2/3 Cup Chopped Dry Roasted
   or Cocktail Peanuts
4 (2.07 oz.) Chocolate Covered
   Peanut, Caramel and
   Nougat Candy Bars,
   Chopped into Small Pieces

1. Preheat oven to 350˚. In a 3-quart heavy saucepan, stir together brown sugar, butter and corn syrup over medium low heat until combined, and butter is melted. Remove from heat and stir in peanut butter, vanilla and egg until mixture is combined. Add flour and oats, and stir until well mixed.

2. Using fingers, press 2/3 of the oat mixture evenly into the bottom of an ungreased 9 x 13 inch baking dish. Set aside. Chill the remaining oat mixture for 30 minutes.

3. Topping: Combine chips, peanut butter and condensed milk in a 2 quart heavy saucepan over medium heat. Stir until chips have melted. Remove from heat and stir in peanuts. Pour mixture evenly over oat crust. Sprinkle chopped candy bars on top. Crumble remaining oat crust mixture over candy.

4. Bake 30-32 minutes, or until golden brown and set. Remove from oven and cool on wire rack. While still slightly warm, use a sharp edge to cut into 48 squares (8 rows x 6 rows).

5. Bars stay fresher if left in pan until served. Cover pan tightly with foil, and store at room temperature up to 3 days, or in the refrigerator up to 1 week. To freeze, wrap cut bars individually in plastic food wrap. Transfer to an airtight container, and freeze up to 4 months.

tip
To chop peanuts, place in a resealable plastic bag and roll over several times with a rolling pin for desired sized pieces (see page 240).

tip
For test purposes, we used Snickers Brand Candy Bars. To chop, use a chef's knife on a cutting board (see page 240).

Variation
Try other flavored candy bars. We successfully tested with Milky Way Brand and Reese's Peanut Butter Cups.

Caution
Do not use a metal pan for baking; it will result in a dry oat base.

Bailey's Brownies

√
Favorite

This decadent caramel topped brownie is a family favorite!

1. Heat oven to 350°. Grease a 9 x 13" glass baking dish with nonstick cooking spray and set aside. Melt the chopped chocolate with the butter, in a 2 quart oven proof saucepan, using the oven method described on page 245. Remove from oven, and stir gently until chocolate and butter are combined and creamy.

2. Add the flour, sugar, baking powder, vanilla, salt and eggs, and stir until well mixed (about 50 strokes). Spread the batter evenly in prepared pan. Bake 15 minutes. Remove from oven.

3. Meanwhile, place caramels and milk in a small sized microwave safe bowl. Microwave on HIGH 2 minutes 15 seconds, stirring every 60 seconds, until creamy and smooth.

4. Drizzle the caramel mixture over the warm brownies until the entire brownie surface is covered. Sprinkle with the chocolate chips, and then the nuts. Return brownies to oven and bake 10-15 minutes, or just until brownies begin to pull away from the sides of the pan. Remove from oven and cool on a wire rack at least 1 hour. Using a sharp edge, cut into 24 squares (6 rows by 4 rows).

5. Brownies stay fresher if left uncut until served. Cover the pan tightly with foil, and store at room temperature for 3 days, or in the refrigerator up to 1 week. To freeze, store between sheets of wax paper in an airtight container for up to 4 months.

8 oz. Sweet Baking Chocolate,
   Broken into Pieces
1/2 Cup Soft Butter
1 1/2 Cups Flour
1 Cup Sugar
1/2 Tsp. Baking Powder
1/2 Tsp. Vanilla
1/4 Tsp. Salt
2 Eggs
1 (14 oz.) Pkg. Caramels
1/3 Cup Milk
1 1/4 Cups Semisweet
   Chocolate Chips
1 Cup Finely Chopped Pecans

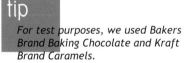

Below 3,500 Feet
Oven: 335°
Flour: Subtract 2 Tbls.
Milk: Subtract 3 Tbls.

tip

For test purposes, we used Bakers Brand Baking Chocolate and Kraft Brand Caramels.

√
Favorite

When you're craving peanut butter and chocolate,
stir together a batch of these quick bars; no mixer needed!

14 oz. Can Sweetened
    Condensed Milk, Divided
1/4 Cup Melted Butter
1/4 Cup Milk
1 (18.25 oz.) Pkg. Devil's Food
    Cake Mix
1 Egg White, Lightly Beaten
7 oz. Jar Marshmallow Cream
2/3 Cup Peanut Butter
    Flavored Chips
1/2 Cup Semisweet Chocolate
    Chips

tip

For test purposes, we used Duncan Hines Brand Devil's Food Cake Mix.

Variation

For more peanut taste, add 1 cup coarsely chopped cocktail or dry roasted peanuts to the marshmallow topping.

tip

Bars are sticky; for clean edges while cutting, spray the cutting edge with nonstick cooking spray, and wipe it with wet paper towels as needed.

1. Preheat oven to 350°. Lightly grease a 9 x 13 inch baking dish with nonstick cooking spray; set aside.

2. Combine 1 cup condensed milk, butter, milk, dry cake mix and egg white in a medium sized mixing bowl. Stir until well combined. Batter will be thick. Using a spreader, spread two-thirds of the batter evenly into prepared pan (layer will be thin).

3. Bake 12 minutes. Remove from oven and cool on a wire rack. Meanwhile, combine remaining condensed milk and marshmallow cream in a medium sized mixing bowl. Stir in chips. Using a spoon, dollop marshmallow mixture evenly over warm brownie layer. Carefully drop remaining chocolate batter by spoonfuls over marshmallow mixture. Using a spreader, carefully swirl mixture, just to level it in the pan. Bake 25-28 minutes, or until marshmallow mixture is golden brown on top. Cool bars on a wire rack.

4. While bars are still slightly warm, use a sharp edge to cut into 32 brownies (8 rows by 4 rows). Let cool completely.

5. Bars stay fresher if left in pan until served. Cover pan tightly with foil, and store at room temperature up to 3 days, or in the refrigerator up to 10 days. Do not freeze.

Caution

Use a glass baking dish; it will result in a more moist brownie.

√ Favorite

Just seven ingredients make this delicious no-bake brownie simple to make!

1. Line a 9-inch square pan with foil, leaving a 2-inch overhang on 2 sides. Generously grease with butter and set aside.

2. Combine chocolate chips and 1 1/4 cups evaporated milk in a 2 quart heavy saucepan. Cook and stir over low heat, until chips melt. Set melted chocolate mixture aside.

3. In a large mixing bowl, combine vanilla wafer crumbs, marshmallows, powdered sugar, salt and peanuts. Stir until blended. Reserve 3/4 cup melted chocolate mixture for the top of brownie. Add remaining melted chocolate mixture to the crumb mixture. Stir until well combined. Using fingers, press evenly into the bottom of prepared pan.

4. Add 1 teaspoon remaining evaporated milk to reserved melted chocolate mixture. Stir until smooth. Spread evenly over chocolate crumb mixture. Chill in pan 1 hour, or until chocolate is set.

5. When chocolate has set up, remove brownies from pan using foil edges to lift. Transfer to a flat cutting surface. Remove foil, and using a sharp edge, cut into 36 pieces (6 rows by 6 rows).

6. Store cut bars between sheets of wax paper in an airtight container at room temperature for 3 days, or in the refrigerator up to 10 days. Do not freeze.

2 Cups Semisweet Chocolate Chips
12 oz. Can Evaporated Milk
3 Cups Vanilla Wafer Crumbs (About 12 oz.)
2 1/2 Cups Miniature Marshmallows
1 Cup Sifted Powdered Sugar
1/2 Tsp. Salt
1 Cup Chopped Cocktail or Dry Roasted Peanuts

tip
To make vanilla wafer crumbs, place whole cookies in a resealable plastic bag, and roll over several times with a rolling pin until crumbly (see page 240).

Caution
The brownie will have a coarse texture, if you don't sift the powdered sugar.

tip
To chop peanuts, use a chef's knife on a cutting board (see page 240).

Variation
Substitute pecans or walnuts for the peanuts.

✓
Favorite

You'll love the easy preparation, and the
luscious flavor of these soft cherry-filled dessert bars.

1 1/2 Cups Sugar
1 Cup Soft Butter
4 Eggs
2 Cups Flour
1 1/2 Tbls. Lemon Juice
1/3 Cup Milk
1 (20 oz.) Can Cherry Pie
    Filling
Sifted Powdered Sugar

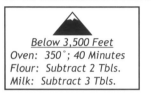

Below 3,500 Feet
Oven: 350˚; 40 Minutes
Flour: Subtract 2 Tbls.
Milk: Subtract 3 Tbls.

tip
Use a Sifter to evenly sprinkle
the bars with powdered sugar.

1. Preheat oven to 350˚. Grease a 9 x 13 inch baking pan (not glass dish) with nonstick cooking spray. Lightly dust with flour, and set aside.

2. In a large mixing bowl, combine sugar and butter. Beat at medium speed until well combined, scraping sides of bowl often. Add eggs, one at a time, beating well after each addition, and continue beating 1 minute until mixture is light and fluffy. At low speed, add flour, lemon juice and milk. Mix well.

3. Spread batter into prepared pan. With a knife, mark off into 15 squares (5 rows by 3 rows). Place 1 heaping tablespoon pie filling in the center of each square. Bake 45-50 minutes, or until golden brown around the edges, and a toothpick inserted in the center comes out clean. Cool completely on a wire rack. Sprinkle with powdered sugar.

4. Bars stay fresher if left uncut until served. Cover pan tightly with foil, and store at room temperature up to 3 days, or in the refrigerator up to 10 days. Do not freeze.

Glenns Ferry Galaxy Squares

✓ Favorite

These pretty bars are a bit time consuming to make - - but the results are "out of this world"!

1. Preheat oven to 350°. Grease a 10 x 15 x 1 inch jelly roll pan with nonstick cooking spray, and set aside. In a large mixing bowl, beat butter and almond paste at medium speed, until mixture is smooth. Add sugar and eggs, and beat well, scraping sides of bowl often. Combine flour and salt; gradually add to almond mixture, alternating with milk, until mixture is well combined. Reserve 1 cup of the dough.

2. Spread remaining dough in prepared pan. Use your fingers to push the dough out to the sides and into the corners, then use a mini rolling pin to even out the dough (see page 239). Open jars of fruit spread. Discard lids. Microwave the fruit spread (in jars) 60 seconds at 30% power. Using a pastry brush, brush warm fruit evenly over dough in pan; spreading 1 flavor on each half of the pan. Chill for 20 minutes.

3. Roll the 1 cup reserved dough with a small rolling pin on a lightly floured surface. Cut the dough into shapes using 2 different 2-inch cookie cutters (we used stars and moons). Place cutouts over fruit spread (stars on one half, moons on the other). Bake on lower oven rack 40 minutes, or until lightly browned. Let cool, and using a sharp edge, cut into 30 squares (6 rows by 5 rows). Bars stay fresher if left uncut until served.

4. Cover pan tightly with foil, and store at room temperature up to 3 days, or in the refrigerator up to 1 week. To freeze, cut bars and wrap individually in plastic food wrap. Transfer to an airtight container and freeze up to 4 months.

1/2 Cup Soft Butter
8 oz. Almond Paste
1 Cup Sugar
2 Eggs
3 1/4 Cups Flour
1/2 Tsp. Salt
1/4 Cup Milk
2 (10 oz.) Jars Fruit Spread;
    Use 2 Different Flavors

Below 3,500 Feet
Oven: 350°; 35 Minutes
Flour: Subtract 1/4 Cup
Milk: Subtract 2 Tbls.

tip
Almond paste can be purchased in tubes or cans, in the baking aisle of your supermarket, located near the canned pie fillings.

tip
For test purposes, we used Smuckers Brand Simply Fruit Red Raspberry and Black Raspberry Spreadable Fruit.

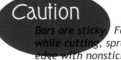

Caution
Bars are sticky. For clean edges while cutting, spray the cutting edge with nonstick cooking spray and wipe it with paper towels as needed.

Redstone Twinkle Bars

2 Dozen Dessert Bars

✓
Favorite

These moist cranberry cheesecake bars make a delightful dessert at your next dinner party!

2 Cups Flour
1 1/2 Cups Quick Cooking Oats
2/3 Cup Packed Brown Sugar
1 Cup Melted Butter
2 Cups Premier White Baking
    Chips
12 oz. Soft Cream Cheese
2 Eggs
14 oz. Can Sweetened
    Condensed Milk
1/4 Cup Lemon Juice
1 Tsp. Vanilla
16 oz. Can Whole Berry
    Cranberry Sauce
2 Tbls. Cornstarch

tip

For test purposes, we used Nestle Brand Premier White Baking Chips.

Variation

Add 1/2 Cup Finely Chopped Nuts to the Topping.

1. Preheat oven to 350°. Lightly grease a 9 x 13 inch baking dish with nonstick cooking spray, and set aside.

2. Combine flour, oats and brown sugar in a large bowl. Add butter, and mix until well combined. Stir in chips. Reserve 2 1/4 cups oat mixture for topping. Firmly press the remaining mixture into prepared pan.

3. Combine cream cheese and eggs in a medium sized mixing bowl. Beat until creamy, scraping sides of bowl often (about 1 minute). Add sweetened condensed milk, lemon juice and vanilla extract. Beat until smooth. Pour over crust. Combine the cranberry sauce and cornstarch in a medium sized bowl. Stir until well mixed. Dollop over cream cheese mixture. Sprinkle reserved oat mixture on top.

4. Bake 40-45 minutes, or until center is set, and edges are light golden brown. Place on a wire rack to cool completely.

5. Use a sharp edge to cut into 24 bars (6 rows by 4 rows). Bars are best if cut at serving time.

6. Bars stay fresher if left in pan until served. Cover pan tightly with foil, and refrigerate until 30 minutes prior to serving. May be stored in the refrigerator up to 5 days. Do not store at room temperature or freeze.

Caution

Do not use a metal baking pan; it will result in a dry bar.

Glendale Coconut Cobbler Bars

We've created a pastry bar that tastes amazingly like peach blueberry cobbler!

1. Preheat oven to 350˚. Line a 9-inch square pan with foil, leaving a 2-inch overhang on 2 sides. Generously grease with butter and set aside.

2. <u>Crust:</u> Combine all crust ingredients in a large mixing bowl. Beat at low speed, scraping bowl often, until mixture is well combined and crumbly (about 1-2 minutes). Reserve 1 cup of the crust mixture. Using your fingers, press remaining crust mixture evenly into the bottom of prepared pan.

3. <u>Topping:</u> Spoon preserves separately in microwave safe measuring cups. Microwave for 1 minutes 30 seconds at 50% power. This will make them more spreadable. Spread 1 1/2 inch wide strips of preserves, side by side, alternating flavors, to within 1/4 inch of edge of crust. Use a knife, to slightly blend preserves together (to give a marbled effect). Sprinkle with reserved crust mixture, and then coconut. Cover loosely with foil, and bake 18 minutes. Remove foil, and bake another 10-12 minutes, or until coconut and edges are lightly browned. Remove and cool in pan on wire rack.

4. When bars have completely cooled, use a sharp edge to cut into 16 bars (4 rows by 4 rows).

5. Bars stay fresher if left uncut until served. Cover pan tightly with foil, and store at room temperature up to 3 days, or in the refrigerator up to 10 days. Do not freeze.

Crust:
1 1/2 Cups Flour
1 Cup Quick Cooking Rolled
    Oats
1/2 Cup Sugar
1/2 Cup Packed Brown Sugar
1/2 Tsp. Baking Soda
1/2 Tsp. Salt
3/4 Cup Melted Butter
1 Tbls. Lemon Juice

Topping:
2/3 Cup Peach Preserves
2/3 Cup Blueberry Preserves
1/2 Cup Sweetened Flaked
    Coconut

tip
To line a pan with foil without tearing it, invert the pan and shape the foil over the bottom. Lift the shaped foil off, and fit it into the upright pan, pressing it gently into the corners (see page 238).

tip
For test purposes, we used Smuckers Brand Peach and Blueberry Preserves.

Variation
These bars are delicious served warm with vanilla ice cream.

☑ Favorite

🕐 Quick n' Easy

A buttery sweet shortbread base peeks out of these cherry chocolate coconut filled squares.

1 Cup Soft Butter
1 1/4 Cups Sugar
1 Egg
1 Tsp. Vanilla
1/2 Cup Milk
2 Tbls. Cherry Juice (From Jar of Maraschino Cherries)
2 1/2 Cups Flour
1 1/2 Tsp. Baking Powder
1/2 Tsp. Salt
1 Cup Semisweet Chocolate Chips
1/2 Cup Finely Chopped Walnuts or Pecans
1/2 Cup Maraschino Cherries, Drained and Chopped
1/2 Cup Sweetened Flaked Coconut

1. Preheat oven to 375°. Generously grease a 10 x 15 x 1 inch jelly roll pan with butter. Dust with flour and set aside.

2. Combine butter and sugar in a large mixing bowl, and beat until creamy, scraping sides of bowl often (about 1 minute). Beat in egg and vanilla. Add milk and cherry juice, and blend well (about 1 more minute). Combine flour, baking powder and salt; gradually add to creamed mixture until well mixed.

3. Fold in chips, nuts, cherries and coconut (mixture will be thick). Use a spreader to evenly distribute the batter into prepared pan. Bake 23-25 minutes, or until lightly browned. Cool in pan on wire rack. Use a sharp edge to cut bars into 40 pieces (8 rows by 5 rows).

4. Bars stay fresher if left uncut until served. Cover pan tightly with foil, and store at room temperature up to 3 days, or in the refrigerator up to 1 week. To freeze, cut bars and wrap individually in plastic food wrap. Transfer to an airtight container, and freeze up to 4 months.

Below 3,500 Feet
Oven: 350°
Flour: Subtract 1/4 Cup
Milk: Subtract 1/4 Cup

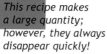

tip

This recipe makes a large quantity; however, they always disappear quickly!

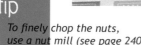

tip

To finely chop the nuts, use a nut mill (see page 240).

Larkspur Lemon Bars

*Lots of fresh lemon juice gives these unique
cream cheese bars their rich flavor.*

1. Preheat oven to 350°. Grease a 9 x 13 inch glass baking dish with nonstick cooking spray. Chop walnuts in a nut mill and set aside.

2. In a medium sized mixing bowl, stir together flour, brown sugar and 1/4 cup sugar. Cut in butter with a pastry blender, until mixture resembles coarse crumbs. Stir in oats and nuts. Reserve about 1 cup of the mixture, and press the remaining crumb mixture into the bottom of the prepared pan.

3. In a small mixing bowl, beat cream cheese, egg, remaining 1/4 cup sugar, lemon juice and food coloring until smooth and creamy. Spread over crust, and sprinkle with reserved crumb mixture.

4. Bake 28-30 minutes, or until edges are a light golden brown. Remove from oven and set on a wire rack to cool completely. Using a sharp edge, cut into 21 bars (7 rows by 3 rows).

5. Bars stay fresher if left uncut until served. Cover pan tightly with foil, and refrigerate up to 10 days. Let sit at room temperature for 20 minutes before cutting and serving.

1 1/2 Cups Flour
1/2 Cup Packed Brown Sugar
1/2 Cup Sugar, Divided
1 Cup Cold Butter
1 Cup Quick Cooking Rolled Oats
2/3 Cup Finely Chopped Walnuts
8 oz. Soft Cream Cheese
1 Egg
1/4 Cup Lemon Juice (Fresh is Best; About 2 Lemons)
3 Drops Yellow Food Coloring

tip *To extract the most juice from a lemon, roll it with your hand on the counter, and then microwave it on HIGH for 20 40 seconds before cutting and squeezing.*

tip *For clean edges in cutting bars, spray the cutting edge with nonstick cooking spray.*

✓ Favorite

Apple n' spice n' everything nice - -
These moist apple nut squares are amazin'!

1 3/4 Cups Flour
1 1/2 Cups Sugar
1 Cup Quick Cooking or Old
      Fashioned Rolled Oats
1 Tsp. Baking Soda
1 1/2 Tsp. Cinnamon
1/2 Tsp. Salt
1/2 Tsp. Nutmeg
1/4 Tsp. Ground Cloves
1 Cup Mayonnaise
1/4 Cup Milk
2 Large Eggs
1 Tsp. Vanilla
2 Cups Peeled and Chopped
      Granny Smith Apples
      (About 2 Apples)
1 Cup Coarsely Chopped
      Pecans

Icing:
4 oz. Soft Cream Cheese
1/2 Cup Soft Butter
3 Cups Sifted Powdered Sugar
1 Tsp. Vanilla
1/4 Cup or More Half n' Half

1. Preheat oven to 375°. Grease a 9 x 13 inch baking dish with nonstick cooking spray. Lightly dust with flour and set aside.

2. In a large mixing bowl, combine flour, sugar, oats, baking soda, cinnamon, salt, nutmeg and cloves. Stir until well combined. In a large sized measuring cup, combine mayonnaise, milk, eggs and vanilla. Whisk until smooth, and add to dry ingredients. Beat at low speed for 2 minutes, or until blended (batter will be slightly thick).

3. Stir in apples and nuts. Spoon batter evenly into prepared baking dish. Bake 30-32 minutes, or until toothpick inserted in center comes out clean. Cool completely in pan on wire rack.

4. Combine all icing ingredients in a medium sized mixing bowl. Beat on high speed until smooth and creamy (1-2 minutes). Spread icing evenly on cooled bars. Using a sharp edge, cut into 24 bars (6 rows by 4 rows).

5. Bars stay fresher if left uncut until served. Cover pan tightly with foil, and store at room temperature up to 3 days, or in the refrigerator up to 1 week. Unfrosted bars freeze well. Cut unfrosted bars and wrap individually in plastic food wrap. Transfer to an airtight container and freeze up to 4 months. Thaw at room temperature and frost. Serve immediately.

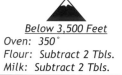

Below 3,500 Feet
Oven: 350°
Flour: Subtract 2 Tbls.
Milk: Subtract 2 Tbls.

tip
Don't hesitate to leave the peel on the apple ; it saves time and adds nutrition.

tip
To save time, purchase chopped pecans in the bag.

Caution
Do not use a metal pan for this recipe; it will result in a dry bar.

Kootenai Kandy Bars

✓
Favorite

*This is a blonde brownie version of
the confection called "turtle".*

1. Preheat oven to 350°. Grease a 9 x 13 inch baking dish with nonstick cooking spray and set aside.

2. In a large mixing bowl, combine 2/3 cup evaporated milk, cake mix and melted butter. Mix until well combined. Spread half the mixture evenly in the prepared pan. Bake 5 minutes and immediately remove from oven. Meanwhile, combine 3 tablespoons evaporated milk and caramels in a small sized microwave safe bowl. Microwave on HIGH 2 minutes 15 seconds, stirring every 60 seconds, or until smooth.

3. Drizzle melted caramel evenly over warm crust. Sprinkle toffee chips, chopped pecans and chocolate chips evenly over caramel. Dollop remaining crust mixture evenly on top, then spread to evenly cover. Return to oven and bake 26-28 minutes, or until light golden brown around edges. Cool completely in pan on wire rack. Use a sharp edge to cut into 24 bars (6 rows by 4 rows).

4. Bars stay fresher if left uncut until served. Cover pan tightly with foil, and store at room temperature up to 3 days, or in the refrigerator up to 1 week. To freeze, cut bars and wrap individually in plastic food wrap. Transfer to an airtight container, and freeze up to 4 months.

14 oz. Pkg. Caramels
12 oz. Can Evaporated Milk, Divided
1 (18.25 oz.) Pkg. White Cake Mix
1/2 Cup Melted Butter
3/4 Cup Milk Chocolate Toffee Bits
1 Cup Coarsely Chopped Pecans
1 Cup Semisweet Chocolate Chips

tip
To coarsely chop pecans, use a chef's knife on a cutting board (see page 240).

tip
For test purposes, we used Kraft Brand Caramels, Duncan Hines Brand White Cake Mix and Heath Brand Milk Chocolate Toffee Bits.

Caution
Do not use a metal pan for this recipe. It will result in a dry bar.

A Gift From The Heart...

Bake a batch of cookies,
and place a dozen on a decorative plate.
Deliver to a friend, with a hand written note inside,
expressing things you appreciate about the friend
and your friendship.

Cookies Galore

This treasured collection of cookies combines
chocolates, nuts, coconut, fruit and spices,
for an unforgettable experience in cookie making.

We've even included a recipe for man's best friend!

*A touch of white and milk chocolate brings these
butterscotch spice cookies to life!*

1/2 Cup Soft Butter
1/2 Cup Buttered Flavored
   Shortening
1 Cup Packed Brown Sugar
2 Eggs
3 Cups Flour
2 (3.5 oz.) Pkg. Cook-and-
   Serve Butterscotch
   Pudding Mix
2 Tsp. Cinnamon
1 Tsp. Ground Ginger
1 Tsp. Baking Powder
1/3 Cup Milk
4 oz. White Chocolate
4 oz. Milk Chocolate
Graduated Sized Cookie
   Cutters

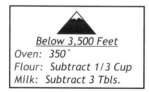

Below 3,500 Feet
Oven: 350°
Flour: Subtract 1/3 Cup
Milk: Subtract 3 Tbls.

tip

*Most discount stores
sell graduated sized
cookie cutter sets.*

tip

*For less mess, use a silicone
mat for rolling out dough
(see page 240). It has a
non-stick surface and is easy
to clean (just wipe with a
clean, damp sponge).*

1. Preheat oven to 375°. In a large mixing bowl, cream butter, shortening and brown sugar. Add eggs and beat well. Combine the flour, pudding mix, cinnamon, ginger and baking powder in a small bowl. Gradually add to creamed mixture, alternating with the milk, until well combined. Cover dough with plastic wrap and chill 1 hour.

2. On a lightly floured surface, roll out dough to 1/4 inch thickness. Cut with varied sized floured cookie cutters. Place cutouts 1 inch apart on ungreased baking sheets. Bake 11-14 minutes, or until edges are golden brown. Remove to wax paper lined wire racks to cool completely.

3. Melt chocolates separately in 1 quart oven proof saucepans, using the oven method described on page 245. Dip the tips of cookies in chocolate. Shake off excess, and place on a wax paper lined baking sheet to set (about 2 hours).

4. Do not cover chocolate until it has dried completely. Store between sheets of wax paper in an airtight tin or foil covered container at room temperature for up to 1 week, or in the refrigerator up to 10 days. Uncoated cookies keep 4 months in the freezer. Thaw at room temperature, then dip in chocolates.

Palmer's Peanut Dippers

✓
Favorite

*These tender, rich shortbread cookies team the
unbeatable taste combination of peanut butter and chocolate!*

1. Preheat oven to 375°. Lightly grease a 10 x 15 x 1 inch baking pan with nonstick cooking spray; set aside. Combine butter, peanut butter, sugar and vanilla in a large bowl. Beat at medium speed, scraping bowl often, until creamy (about 1-2 minutes). Reduce speed to low; add flour. Beat just until mixture forms a dough. Stir in miniature chocolate chips and peanuts by hand. Using your fingers, pat dough evenly into prepared baking pan, making sure to spread dough evenly and to all edges. Use a mini rolling pin to even out the dough in the pan (see page 239).

2. Bake 18-20 minutes, or until set and lightly browned. Using a sharp edge, immediately cut into 45 pieces (9 rows by 6 rows). Cool completely, then score again before removing cookies from pan.

3. Melt the chocolate in a 1 quart oven proof saucepan using the oven method described on page 245. Dip top half of cooled cookies into chocolate and place on wax paper lined wire rack to set up (about 2 hours).

4. Do not cover chocolate until it has dried completely. Store cookies between sheets of wax paper in an airtight tin, or foil covered container in a cool, dry place for up to 10 days. Do not store in the refrigerator. Undipped cookies keep 4 months in your freezer. Thaw at room temperature, then dip in chocolate.

3/4 Cup Soft Butter
1/2 Cup Creamy Peanut Butter
1 Cup Sugar
1 Tsp. Vanilla
2 Cups Flour
3/4 Cup Miniature Semisweet
  Chocolate Chips
1/2 Cup Finely Chopped Dry
  Roasted or Cocktail
  Peanuts

Coating:
8 oz. Milk Chocolate

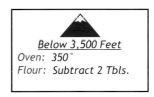

Below 3,500 Feet
Oven: 350°
Flour: Subtract 2 Tbls.

tip

To measure peanut butter, pour 1/2 cup water into a 1 cup sized measuring cup. Then, add peanut butter until the water line reaches the 1 cup line. Drain the water and add the peanut butter to the recipe.

tip

To finely chop peanuts, place in a resealable plastic bag and roll over several times with a rolling pin for desired sized pieces (see page 240).

Bozeman Buckthorn Cookies

4 Dozen Cookies

☑ Favorite   🕐 Quick n' Easy

You will satisfy your craving for a candy bar in just one or two bites of this cookie.

1/3 Cup Butter Flavored
    Shortening
1/3 Cup Soft Butter
1/2 Cup Creamy Peanut Butter
2/3 Cup Packed Brown Sugar
1/2 Cup Sugar
1 Tsp. Baking Soda
1/2 Tsp. Salt
2 Eggs
1/3 Cup Milk
1 Tsp. Vanilla
2 1/4 Cups Flour
3/4 Cup Milk Chocolate Chips
3/4 Cup Honey-Roasted
    Peanuts
48 Miniature Peanut Butter
    Cups, Unwrapped
    (About 14 oz.)

1. Preheat oven to 375°. In a large mixing bowl, beat the shortening, butter and peanut butter until creamy (about 1 minute). Add sugars, baking soda and salt. Beat until combined, scraping sides of the bowl often.

2. Add eggs, milk and vanilla and beat until creamy. Reduce speed to low and beat in as much of the flour as you can with the mixer. Stir in the remaining flour, chocolate chips and peanuts with a wooden spoon until well combined.

3. Using a small cookie scoop (see page 239), drop dough by rounded scoopfuls 2 inches apart onto ungreased baking sheets. Bake 10 minutes, or until lightly browned. Immediately press a peanut butter cup into the center of each warm cookie, and let sit on the hot baking sheet for 3 minutes. Remove to wax paper lined wire racks to cool completely.

4. Store between sheets of wax paper in an airtight container at room temperature for up to 3 days, in the refrigerator up to 10 days, or in the freezer up to 4 months.

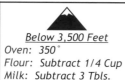

Below 3,500 Feet
Oven: 350°
Flour: Subtract 1/4 Cup
Milk: Subtract 3 Tbls.

tip
For test purposes, we used Reese's Brand Miniature Peanut Butter Cups.

tip
To measure peanut butter, pour 1/2 cup water into a 1 cup sized measuring cup. Then, add peanut butter until the water line reaches the 1 cup line. Drain the water and add the peanut butter to the recipe.

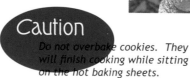

Caution
Do not overbake cookies. They will finish cooking while sitting on the hot baking sheets.

Variation
Substitute other Miniature Candy Bars in the Center; we successfully tested with Snickers and Milky Way Brands.

Jefferson's Turtle Dip Cookies

✓
Favorite

*We've reinvented the popular turtle candy
into a rich, buttery caramel coated cookie!*

1. In a large bowl, combine brown sugar, butter and shortening. Beat until light and fluffy. Add vanilla, maple flavoring and eggs. Beat until smooth and creamy, scraping sides of bowl often. Add flour, baking soda, milk and salt. Mix well. Cover bowl with plastic wrap, and chill 1 hour.

2. Preheat oven to 375˚. Grease baking sheets with nonstick cooking spray and set aside. Arrange pecan pieces in groups of 5 on prepared baking sheets to resemble head and legs of a turtle.

3. In a small bowl, beat egg white and water until frothy. Using a small cookie scoop (see page 239), shape dough into 1 inch balls, then coat in egg white mixture. Press dough ball lightly onto pecans (tips of pecans should still show). Bake 12-14 minutes, or until puffed and golden brown. Immediately remove to wax paper lined wire racks to cool completely.

4. Place caramels and half n' half in a small sized microwave safe bowl. Microwave on HIGH 1 minute 30 seconds, stirring every 30 seconds. Meanwhile, melt the chocolate in a 1 quart oven proof saucepan using the oven method described on page 245. Place 1 teaspoon melted caramel on top of each cookie. Cool to set (about 10 minutes). Frost top of caramel and cookie with melted chocolate. Let set (about 2 hours).

5. Do NOT cover chocolate until it has dried completely. Store between sheets of wax paper in an airtight tin or foil covered container at room temperature for up to 1 week. Refrigerate up to 2 weeks. Do not freeze.

1 Cup Packed Brown Sugar
1/2 Cup Soft Butter
1/2 Cup Butter Flavored
    Shortening
1 Tsp. Vanilla
1/4 Tsp. Imitation Maple
    Flavoring
3 Eggs
3 1/4 Cups Flour
1 1/4 Tsp. Baking Soda
1/3 Cup Milk
1 Tsp. Salt
1 Cup Pecan Halves, Split
    Lengthwise
1 Egg White plus 1 Tsp. Water

<u>Topping:</u>
7 oz. Caramels
2 Tsp. Half n' Half
8 oz. Milk Chocolate

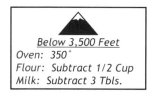
Below 3,500 Feet
Oven: 350˚
Flour: Subtract 1/2 Cup
Milk: Subtract 3 Tbls.

tip
For test purposes, we used Kraft Brand Caramels and Hershey's Brand Milk Chocolate Bars.

Caution
Do not frost cookie with chocolate until caramel has set up; if necessary, refrigerate cookie for 5-10 minutes.

✓
Favorite

*We've reinvented the German Chocolate Cake --
into a delightful chocolate coconut frosted cookie!*

1/2 Cup Soft Butter
1 Cup Sugar
2 Eggs
1 Tsp. Vanilla
1 Cup Flour
1/2 Tsp. Baking Powder
1/2 Tsp. Salt
1/2 Cup Unsweetened Cocoa
    Powder

Frosting:
3/4 Cup Sugar
1/2 Cup Light Corn Syrup
1/2 Cup Evaporated Milk
1/2 Cup Soft Butter
3 Beaten Egg Yolks
1 Tsp. Vanilla
1 1/3 Cups Sweetened Flaked
    Coconut
1 Cup Coarsely Chopped
    Pecans

tip

*To chop pecans, use a chef's knife
and a cutting board (see page 240).*

tip

*Store nuts in the freezer
for optimum freshness,
and always taste them
before adding to your
recipes.*

1. Preheat oven to 350˚. Lightly grease baking sheets with nonstick cooking spray; set aside.

2. Combine butter, sugar, eggs and vanilla in a medium sized mixing bowl and beat until creamy, scraping sides of bowl often. Combine all dry ingredients and add to the mixture. Beat until well combined. Chill dough for 30 minutes. Using a small cookie scoop (see page 239), drop batter by rounded scoopfuls 2 inches apart onto prepared baking sheets. Bake 10-12 minutes, or until firm. Remove from oven, and let sit on hot baking sheet for 1 more minute. Remove to wax paper lined wire racks to cool completely.

3. Frosting: Combine all ingredients except coconut and pecans in a 2 quart heavy saucepan. Cook over medium high heat, stirring constantly with a wooden spoon, until mixture comes to a low boil. Reduce heat to medium low, and cook, stirring constantly, 10-12 minutes. Remove from heat and stir in coconut and pecans. Cool for 15 minutes, or until thick enough to spread.

4. Spread frosting on cooled cookies. Let set (about 30 minutes).

5. Store between sheets of wax paper in an airtight container at room temperature for up to 1 week, or in the refrigerator up to 2 weeks. Unfrosted cookies keep 4 months in your freezer. Thaw at room temperature, then frost.

√
Favorite

*Sweet chocolate morsels hide inside these
powdered sugar coated cookies.*

1. Preheat oven to 375˚. To finely chop the nuts, use a nut mill (see page 240). Set aside.

2. Combine butter, sugar, vanilla and salt in a large mixing bowl. Beat until creamy (about 1 minute), scraping sides of bowl often. Gradually add flour and mix just until combined. Stir in chocolate chips and nuts. Dough will be crumbly.

3. Using a small cookie scoop (see page 239), drop rounded scoopfuls of dough into your hand and compress to shape into balls. Place 2 inches apart on ungreased baking sheets.

4. Bake 14 minutes, or until cookies are set and lightly browned on the bottoms. Remove and place on wax paper lined wire racks. While cookies are still warm, roll in powdered sugar 3 or 4 times until evenly coated. Cool completely, then roll in powdered sugar one more time.

5. Store between sheets of wax paper in an airtight container at room temperature for up to 1 week, or in the refrigerator up to 10 days. Do not freeze.

1 1/2 Cups Soft Butter
3/4 Cup Powdered Sugar
1 Tbls. Vanilla
1/2 Tsp. Salt
3 Cups Flour
**12 oz. Miniature Semisweet
   Chocolate Chips**
**1/2 Cup Finely Chopped
   Walnuts**
Sifted Powdered Sugar

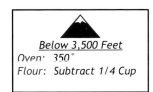

Below 3,500 Feet
Oven: 350˚
Flour: Subtract 1/4 Cup

Variation
*Try substituting pecans
for the walnuts.*

*These delicious chocolate and pecan cookies are easy to make --
all you do is add filling to frozen puff pastry, and bake!*

5 oz. Semisweet Baking
    Chocolate
1 Cup Finely Chopped Toasted
    Pecans
1/2 Cup Superfine Sugar
1 Tsp. Cinnamon
17 oz. Frozen Puff Pastry
    Dough, Thawed (2 Sheets)

**Extra Superfine Sugar for
Rolling Puff Pastry**

Below 3,500 Feet
Oven: 400˚

---

tip

*To toast pecans, arrange whole nuts in a
single layer on a foil-lined baking sheet
in a 350˚ oven for 8-10 minutes,
stirring 2 or 3 times until desired flavor
is reached. Cool completely, then to
finely chop, using a nut mill (see page
240).*

tip

*For test purposes, we used
Pepperidge Farm Brand Puff
Pastry Sheets and Baker's
Brand Semisweet Baking
Chocolate.*

Variation

*Any type nut can be
substituted for the
pecans.*

Caution

*Chocolate and nut mixtures should be
spread thin and evenly, to allow ease in
rolling up the dough.*

1. Preheat oven to 425˚. Lightly grease baking sheets with nonstick cooking spray and set aside. Microwave baking chocolate in a microwave safe measuring cup at 80% power for 4 minutes, stirring every 60 seconds. Set aside.

2. In a small bowl, combine pecans, sugar and cinnamon. Generously sprinkle working surface with extra superfine sugar, and roll out each puff pastry sheet to a rectangle about 9 x 12 inches in size. Spread half the chocolate on each sheet to within 1 inch of all edges. Sprinkle half of the cinnamon nut mixture on each sheet.

3. Roll up one long side of each dough sheet to the center, then roll up the other side so they meet in the center. Where the pieces meet, dampen the edges with a little water, to join them. Use a sharp knife to cut off raw edges, then cut dough log into 1/2 inch slices. Place 2 inches apart on prepared baking sheets. Bake 13-14 minutes, or until golden brown. Transfer to wax paper lined wire racks to cool completely.

4. Store between sheets of wax paper in an airtight tin, or foil covered container in a cool, dry place for up to 5 days, or in the refrigerator up to 2 weeks. Cookies keep 3 months in your freezer.

Favorite

Our favorite scone recipe transformed into a delicate cake-soft cookie; the creamy buttermilk icing makes them impossible to resist!

1. Preheat oven to 375°. Grease baking sheets with nonstick cooking spray. In a large bowl, combine flour, sugar, baking powder and salt. Add butter and cream cheese, and stir just enough to combine. The dough will be lumpy. Add egg and buttermilk and stir until the dough forms a ball. Do not over mix, as dough will toughen.

2. Add dried cranberries and nuts, and again stir just enough to combine. Roll the dough with a mini floured rolling pin (see page 239) on a lightly floured surface, to 1/2 inch thickness. Always roll from the center to the edges.

3. Cut the dough into shapes using floured 2-inch cookie cutters, cutting as close together as possible. Place cutouts 2 inches apart on prepared baking sheets. Bake 16-18 minutes, or until light golden brown on the edges. Remove to wax paper lined wire rack to cool completely.

4. Icing: Chop nuts in a nut mill (see page 240). Combine buttermilk and butter in a small saucepan over medium heat. Bring to a gentle boil and remove. Add powdered sugar and vanilla and beat until smooth. Frost cooled cookies and immediately sprinkle nuts on top. Store between sheets of wax paper in an airtight container at room temperature for up to 3 days, or in the refrigerator up to 1 week. Do not freeze.

3 Cups Flour
1/2 Cup Sugar
1 Tbls. Baking Powder
1/2 Tsp. Salt
3/4 Cup Soft Butter
4 oz. Soft Cream Cheese
1 Egg
3/4 Cup Buttermilk
2/3 Cup Sweetened Dried
   Cranberries
1 Cup Coarsely Chopped
   Walnuts

Icing:
1/4 Cup Soft Butter
1/3 Cup or More Buttermilk
2 1/2 Cups Sifted Powdered
   Sugar
1 Tsp. Vanilla
1/2 Cup Finely Chopped
   Walnuts

Below 3,500 Feet
Oven: 350°
Flour: Subtract 1/3 Cup
Milk: Subtract 1/4 Cup

tip

For test purposes, we used Craisins Brand Sweetened Dried Cranberries.

tip

To chop walnuts, place in a resealable plastic bag and roll over several times with a rolling pin for desired sized pieces (see page 240).

Favorite

This soft chocolate cookie log forms a crackled top as it bakes;
it also tastes great without the white chocolate nut topping.

1 1/2 Cups Packed Brown
  Sugar
2/3 Cup Butter Flavored
  Shortening
2 Tbls. Milk
1 Tsp. Vanilla
2 Eggs
1 2/3 Cups Flour
1/3 Cup Unsweetened Cocoa
  Powder
1 Tsp. Salt
1/2 Tsp. Baking Soda
1 Cup Semisweet Chocolate
  Chips
3/4 Cup Finely Chopped
  Pecans

Drizzled Topping (Optional):
4 oz. White Chocolate
2/3 Cup Finely Chopped
  Pecans

Below 3,500 Feet
Oven: 350˚
Flour: Subtract 2 Tbls.
Milk: Do Not Add Milk

---

tip
For test purposes, we used
Ghiradelli Brand White
Chocolate Baking Bars.

tip

A plastic squeeze bottle can be
used for squeezing melted choc-
olate in lines and patterns over
logs (see page 243). If chocolate
becomes too thick, microwave it
inside the bottle for 15 second
intervals at 30% power.

1. Use a nut mill to finely chop pecans (see page 240). Set aside. Line a large baking sheet with parchment paper (not wax paper). Preheat oven to 350˚.

2. In a large mixing bowl, combine brown sugar, shortening, milk, vanilla and eggs. Beat at medium speed, scraping sides of bowl often, until creamy (about 2 minutes). Add flour, cocoa, salt, baking soda, chocolate chips and 3/4 cup pecans. Beat at medium speed until well combined.

3. Divide dough in half. Shape each half into a 13-inch long by 2 1/2 inch wide log. Place logs 3 inches apart on prepared baking sheet (dough will spread out while baking). Bake 22-24 minutes, or until firm to the touch, and a toothpick inserted in the center, comes out clean (if toothpick inserts inside melted chocolate chip, it will not appear clean). Remove from oven and transfer parchment paper with logs attached, to wire rack to cool completely.

4. Topping (Optional): Melt chocolate in a 1 quart oven proof saucepan using the oven method described on page 245. Transfer to a plastic squeeze bottle and drizzle over cooled cookie logs. Immediately sprinkle with pecans. When ready to serve, use a sharp edge to cut into 1 inch slices.

5. Cookies stay fresher if left uncut until served. Cover with plastic wrap and store at room temperature up to 3 days, or in the refrigerator up to 10 days. Do not freeze.

✓ Favorite

*These soft cookies with a hint of coconut taste so good,
others will have a hard time believing how simple they are to make!*

1. Preheat oven to 375°. In a large mixing bowl, beat the butter about 30 seconds until softened. Add half of the flour. Then add the sugar, egg, milk and vanilla. Beat until thoroughly combined, scraping the sides of the bowl often. Stir in the remaining flour and mix well.

2. Stir in 1 cup coconut. With a small cookie scoop (see page 239), drop dough by rounded scoopfuls onto ungreased baking sheets. Bake 11-13 minutes, or until edges are firm and bottoms are lightly browned.

3. Remove cookies and cool on wax paper lined wire racks. Cool completely, then spread with 1 heaping tablespoonful pink frosting, and immediately top with toasted coconut.

4. Pink Cream Cheese Icing: Beat cream cheese, butter and vanilla together until smooth. Add powdered sugar, half n' half and food coloring and beat until creamy.

5. Store between sheets of wax paper in an airtight container at room temperature for up to 5 days, or in the refrigerator up to 10 days. Unfrosted cookies keep 4 months in your freezer. Thaw at room temperature, then frost and decorate.

1/2 Cup Soft Butter
1 1/2 Cups Flour
3/4 Cup Sugar
1 Egg
1/4 Cup Milk
1 Tsp. Vanilla
1 Cup Sweetened Flaked
   Coconut

Pink Cream Cheese Icing:
4 oz. Soft Cream Cheese
1/4 Cup Soft Butter
2 Cups Sifted Powdered Sugar
1 Tsp. Vanilla
2 Tbls. or More Half n' Half
4 Drops Red Food Coloring
Toasted Sweetened Flaked
   Coconut

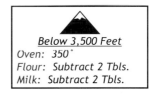

Below 3,500 Feet
Oven: 350°
Flour: Subtract 2 Tbls.
Milk: Subtract 2 Tbls.

tip

To toast coconut, preheat oven to 350°. Spread the coconut in a single layer on a foil lined shallow baking pan. Bake for 8-10 minutes, stirring twice, until light golden brown. The coconut will become crisper as it cools.

*This soft chewy coconut cookie
is surrounded with chocolate and raspberry!*

7 oz. Sweetened Flaked
    Coconut
2/3 Cup Sugar
1/2 Cup Flour
1/2 Tsp. Salt
3 Egg Whites at Room
    Temperature, Lightly
    Beaten
1/2 Tsp. Almond Extract

6 oz. Milk Chocolate
1/3 Cup Raspberry Jam or
    Preserves

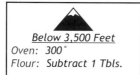

Below 3,500 Feet
Oven: 300˚
Flour: Subtract 1 Tbls.

tip

*Remove eggs from the refrigerator
20-30 minutes before baking.
Remember, eggs separate more
easily when they are COLD.*

tip

*For test purposes, we used
Hershey's Brand Milk Chocolate
Bars, and Smucker's Brand
Raspberry Preserves.*

Variation

*This cookie can be filled
with any flavor preserves.*

Caution

*Do not store cookies until
chocolate has dried
completely; otherwise
chocolate will absorb
moisture, and separate.*

1. Preheat oven to 325˚. Line baking sheets with parchment paper, and set aside.

2. In a large sized mixing bowl, combine coconut, sugar, flour and salt. Stir until well combined. In a separate small bowl, beat egg whites until firm but not stiff. Add almond extract to egg whites and gently combine. Add egg white mixture to coconut mixture, and stir until well mixed. Using a small cookie scoop (see page 239), drop by flat scoopfuls (no overflow batter), 1 inch apart on prepared baking sheets. Lightly flour your thumb or bottom of a melon ball tool, and press into the center of each mound, to make an indentation. Bake 20-22 minutes, or until edges are golden. Remove from oven, and use your thumb or a melon ball tool, to press indentations again. Remove cookies (on parchment sheets) to wire racks to cool completely.

3. Melt chocolate in a 1 quart oven proof saucepan using the oven method described on page 245. Carefully dip the bottom of each cooled cookie into the melted chocolate, letting excess drip off. Place cookies, chocolate coating sides up, on parchment paper; let set (about 1 hour). To fill cookies, just before serving, spoon about
1/2 teaspoon of the jam into the indentation in each cookie.

4. Store between sheets of wax paper in an airtight container in the refrigerator up to 10 days. Do not store at room temperature or freeze. Wait until serving to fill with jam.

Rollinsville Roundies

☑ Favorite

Add some razzle dazzle to your cookie tray by presenting
these raspberry rolled cookies tied in bundles with festive ribbon.

1. Combine butter and sugar in a medium sized mixing bowl. Beat at medium speed until creamy, scraping sides of bowl often. Add egg and vanilla and beat well. Combine flour, baking powder and salt; gradually add to butter mixture with milk, beating well. Shape dough into a roll; wrap tightly in plastic wrap and refrigerate 1 hour.

2. In a small bowl, combine coconut, jam and walnuts; stir until well combined. Roll dough with a lightly floured mini rolling pin (see page 239) on a lightly floured surface to 1/4 inch thickness. Always roll from the center to the edges. Spread coconut filling evenly over dough to within 1/4 inch of edges. Starting at long side, roll up dough tightly; pinching edges to close. Cut the roll in half. Wrap rolls in plastic wrap, and place in the freezer until firm (about 1 hour). At this point, you can freeze the dough for up to 3 days.

3. Preheat oven to 375°. Line baking sheets with parchment paper and set aside. Unwrap dough, and use a sharp knife to cut off loose ends and discard. Then, cut into 1/4 inch thick slices. Place 2 inches apart on prepared baking sheets. Bake 16-18 minutes, or until edges are lightly browned. Remove to wax paper lined wire racks to cool. Use a shaker to lightly dust cooled cookies with powdered sugar.

4. Store between sheets of wax paper in an airtight container at room temperature for up to 5 days, in the refrigerator up to 10 days, or in the freezer up to 4 months.

1/2 Cup Soft Butter
1 Cup Superfine Sugar
1 Egg
1 Tsp. Vanilla
2 1/4 Cups Flour
1 Tsp. Baking Powder
1/2 Tsp. Salt
2 Tbls. Milk
1/2 Cup Sweetened Flaked
   Coconut
2/3 Cup Raspberry Jam
   or Preserves
1/2 Cup Finely Chopped
   Walnuts

Sifted Powdered Sugar

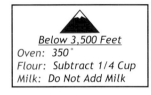

Below 3,500 Feet
Oven: 350°
Flour: Subtract 1/4 Cup
Milk: Do Not Add Milk

tip
Use a nut mill to finely chop walnuts (see page 240).

tip
Superfine sugar blends and dissolves more quickly and evenly than granulated sugar. As a result, you get a smoother texture, and more even browning.

Variation
Substitute your favorite flavor jam or nut in this recipe.

Low Sugar

Savor the flavor of this slice n' bake cookie, bursting with the goodness of cranberries, chocolate and nuts.

1 Cup Soft Butter
1/2 Cup Sugar
1/4 Cup Milk
1 Tsp. Vanilla
1 Tsp. Salt
2 1/2 Cups Flour
3/4 Cup Sweetened Dried
    Cranberries
1/2 Cup Miniature Semisweet
    Chocolate Chips
2/3 Cup Chopped Pecans
1 1/2 Cups Sweetened Flaked
    Coconut

Below 3,500 Feet
Oven: 350˚
Flour: Subtract 1/4 Cup
Milk: Subtract 2 Tbls.

1. In a large bowl, cream butter and sugar until light and fluffy. Add milk, vanilla and salt, and mix just until combined. On low speed, add flour, cranberries, chocolate chips and pecans. Mix until combined, scraping sides of bowl often.

2. Divide the dough in fourths. Knead each section to combine ingredients, and shape into 4 inch logs, about 2 inches in diameter. Place coconut in a shallow bowl, and roll each log in the coconut, pressing on coconut to coat the outside of the log. Wrap each log in plastic wrap and freeze for 1 hour until firm.

3. Preheat oven to 375˚. Using a sharp knife, cut the frozen logs into 1/3 inch thick slices. Transfer to ungreased baking sheets, placing them 1 inch apart. Let sit 5 minutes before baking. Bake 12-14 minutes, or until edges are golden. Transfer to a wax paper lined wire rack to cool completely.

4. Store between sheets of wax paper in an airtight container at room temperature for up to 1 week, in the refrigerator up to 2 weeks, or in the freezer up to 4 months.

tip

You can freeze n' bake the logs by placing the wrapped dough in a resealable freezer bag. There is no need to thaw the dough; just slice n' bake. You may need to add a minute or two to the bake time.

Variation

Try substituting walnuts and raisins for the fruit and nuts.

Low Sugar

A pistachio lover's dream - - nuts inside and out;
the low sugar cookie base is delicious all by itself!

1. Combine butter, shortening and powdered sugar in a medium sized mixing bowl. Beat on medium speed, scraping bowl often, until well mixed. Add egg, and continue beating until combined. Reduce speed to low; add flour, salt and milk, and mix well. Chill dough for 30 minutes.

2. Preheat oven to 375°. Place 3/4 cup chopped pistachios in a shallow bowl. Using a small cookie scoop (see page 239), drop dough by flat scoopfuls (no overflow batter) into the nuts and coat sparingly. Place coated dough balls 2 inches apart on ungreased baking sheets. Flatten each cookie to a 2" diameter circle with the bottom of a glass dipped in sugar. Bake 10-12 minutes, or until edges are lightly browned. Transfer to a wax paper lined wire rack to cool completely.

3. Filling: Transfer frosting to a small mixing bowl. Add food coloring and mix well. Add 1/4 cup chopped pistachio nuts and stir until well combined. It is best to wait until serving time to frost and assemble cookies.

4. For each sandwich cookie, spread about 1 heaping tablespoon frosting onto bottom of 1 cookie; top with second cookie, and squeeze together gently until frosting spreads out over edges of cookies. Store unfrosted cookies between sheets of wax paper in an airtight container for up to 5 days at room temperature, or in the refrigerator up to 10 days. Unfrosted cookies keep 4 months in your freezer. Thaw at room temperature, then frost and assemble.

1/2 Cup Soft Butter
1/4 Cup Butter Flavored
   Shortening
3/4 Cup Powdered Sugar
1 Egg
1 3/4 Cups Flour
1/2 Tsp. Salt
1/4 Cup Milk
3/4 Cup Coarsely Chopped
   Pistachio Nuts

Filling:
16 oz. Container Cream
   Cheese Flavored Frosting
4 Drops Green Food Coloring
1 Drop Yellow Food Coloring
1/4 Cup Coarsely Chopped
   Pistachio Nuts

Below 3,500 Feet
Oven: 350°
Flour: Subtract 1/4 Cup
Milk: Subtract 2 Tbls.

tip

When buying unshelled pistachios, look for ones with the shell partially open, so it's easier to retrieve the nut. To chop, place in a resealable plastic bag and roll over several times with a rolling pin for desired sized pieces (see page 240).

✓

Favorite

Cut-out tree shaped cookies with the unique flavor combination of pistachios and chocolate.

1/2 Cup Soft Butter
1/2 Cup Butter Flavored
    Shortening
3/4 Cup Packed Brown Sugar
1/2 Cup Sugar
1 Tsp. Vanilla
2 Eggs
2 1/2 Cups Flour
1 Tsp. Salt
1 Tsp. Baking Soda
2 Tbls. Milk
3/4 Cup Finely Chopped
    Pistachio Nuts
    (About 4 oz.)

Icing:
1/4 Cup Soft Butter
2 Tbls. Light Corn Syrup
1/4 Cup Half n' Half
4 oz. Unsweetened Baking
    Chocolate, Broken Up
1 Tsp Vanilla
2 Cups Sifted Powdered
    Sugar
3/4 Cup Finely Chopped
    Pistachio Nuts
    (About 4 oz.)

1. Combine butter, shortening, sugars and vanilla in a large mixing bowl. Beat until creamy, scraping sides of bowl often (about 1 minute). Add eggs and beat well. Combine flour, salt and soda, and add to batter with milk, beating at low speed until well mixed. Stir in nuts. Cover and chill dough for 1 hour.

2. Preheat oven to 375˚. Roll half the dough at a time with a floured mini rolling pin (see page 239), on a lightly floured surface to 1/4" thickness. Always roll from the center to the edges. Cut the dough into tree shapes, using a floured 2 1/2" cookie cutter, cutting as close together as possible. Transfer to ungreased baking sheets, placing shapes 1 inch apart. Bake 9-10 minutes, or until edges are light golden brown. Transfer to wax paper lined wire racks to cool completely.

3. Icing: In a 2 quart saucepan, combine butter, corn syrup and half n' half. Cook over medium heat, stirring, until mixture barely comes to a low boil. Remove from heat and add chocolate. Stir until melted. Add vanilla and powdered sugar, and beat until smooth and shiny (about 1 minute), scraping sides of pan often. Frost cookies and immediately sprinkle with nuts.

4. Do NOT cover chocolate until it has dried completely. Store cookies between sheets of wax paper in an airtight tin or foil covered container in a cool, dry place for 3 days, or in the refrigerator up to 2 weeks. Unfrosted cookies keep 4 months in your freezer. Thaw at room temperature, then frost, decorate and serve.

▲

Below 3,500 Feet
Oven: 350˚
Flour: Subtract 1/4 Cup
Milk: Do Not Add Milk

tip

When buying pistachios, look for ones with the shell partially open, so it's easier to retrieve the nut.
To chop, use a chef's knife on a cutting board (see page 240).

Variation

Peanuts are a tasty substitution for the pistachios. Also, try adding 1 cup semisweet chocolate chips to the batter.

Low Sugar   ✓ Favorite

*Tie a large ribbon and name tag around each gift bone;
they've been dog tested and dog approved!*

1. Preheat oven to 325°. In a medium sized mixing bowl, stir together flours, brown sugar, peanuts, sesame seeds, sunflower seeds and wheat germ. Add butter, and beat until well combined. Make a well in the center of the mixture. Add egg and water to well. Continue to beat batter until well mixed.

2. Turn dough onto lightly floured surface. Knead by folding and gently pressing dough 4-6 strokes, or until it holds together. Roll dough with floured mini rolling pin (see page 239) to 1/4" thickness. Use a large sized bone shaped cutter to cut out dough. Place cutouts 1 inch apart onto ungreased baking sheets. Bake 25 minutes, or until golden brown. Turn oven off, and let bones dry in the oven 2 hours (do NOT open oven door).

3. Break almond bark into pieces, and place in a small sized microwave safe bowl. Microwave on HIGH 90 seconds. Stir well. Microwave on HIGH 15 more seconds. Stir again until smooth. If necessary, microwave in 15 second intervals until smooth. Dip top of each bone in almond bark mixture, and immediately sprinkle with nonpareils. Place on a wax paper lined baking sheet to set (about 30 minutes).

4. Store between sheets of wax paper in an airtight container at room temperature for up to 4 weeks. Do not refrigerate or freeze. For gift giving, you can also wrap in plastic bags or colored cellophane.

1 Cup White Flour
3/4 Cup Whole Wheat Flour
1/2 Cup Packed Brown Sugar
1/2 Cup Ground Peanuts
1/4 Cup Sesame Seeds
**1/4 Cup Dry Roasted Sunflower
    Kernels**
2 Tbls. Toasted Wheat Germ
3/4 Cup Soft Butter
1 Egg
1/4 Cup Water
**10 oz. Vanilla Flavored Almond
    Bark Coating**
Multi-Colored Nonpareils

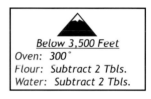

Below 3,500 Feet
Oven: 300°
Flour: Subtract 2 Tbls.
Water: Subtract 2 Tbls.

tip

Nuts stay fresher when stored in a tightly sealed canning jar in the freezer.

tip

Bone cookies will darken a little more as they dry in the oven, so turn the oven off as soon as they are golden.

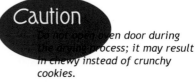

Caution
Do not open oven door during the drying process; it may result in chewy instead of crunchy cookies.

For All Your Furry Friends...

Bake a batch of "Ruthie's Cookie Bones For Dogs"
on page 211.
Wrap a few in colored cellophane with ribbon,
and deliver to all the dog lovers in your life.

Christmas Classics

Head to the kitchen and create happy Holiday
memories by baking and sharing these traditional
treats with family and friends.
This unique collection of cookies from Christmas' past,
will be a keepsake for years to come.

✓
Favorite

These tender, cakey sugar cookies are topped with an irresistible butter rich icing!

1/4 Cup Soft Butter
1/2 Cup Butter Flavored
    Shortening
1 Cup Sugar
2 Eggs
1 Tsp. Vanilla
1/4 Cup Milk
2 1/2 Cups Flour
1 Tsp. Baking Powder
1 Tsp. Salt

Butter Rich Icing:
1/4 Cup Melted Butter
1/2 Tsp. Vanilla
2 Cups Sifted Powdered Sugar
1/4 Cup Half n' Half or Milk
Food Coloring of Choice
Colored Nonpareils

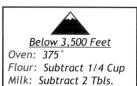

Below 3,500 Feet
Oven: 375˚
Flour: Subtract 1/4 Cup
Milk: Subtract 2 Tbls.

1. In a large mixing bowl, combine butter, shortening, sugar, eggs and vanilla. Beat until well combined (about 1 minute). Add milk, flour, baking powder and salt and beat well. Cover dough and refrigerate 1 hour.

2. Preheat oven to 400˚. Roll the dough with a floured mini rolling pin (see page 239) on a lightly floured surface to 1/4 inch thickness. Always roll from the center to the edges. Cut the dough into shapes using floured 2 1/2" cookie cutters, cutting as close together as possible. Transfer dough to ungreased baking sheets, placing shapes 2 inches apart. Bake 8-10 minutes, or until edges are light brown. Remove to wax paper lined wire racks to cool completely.

3. Icing: Combine all ingredients except nonpareils in a small bowl and beat until creamy. Add more half n' half or milk if necessary for a creamy consistency. Frost cookies and immediately sprinkle with nonpareils.

4. Store between sheets of wax paper in an airtight container at room temperature for up to 1 week, or in the refrigerator up to 10 days. Unfrosted cookies keep 6 months in your freezer. Thaw at room temperature, then frost and decorate.

tip

For less mess, use a pastry mat for rolling out dough (see page 240). It has a non-stick surface and is easy to clean (just wipe with a clean, damp sponge).

tip

In cookie recipes, shortening contributes to a softer-texture and more cake like cookie.

Favorite

*Each irresistible cookie has a spritz texture and taste,
enclosed in a sweet creamy coating.*

1. Preheat oven to 375°. Place butter in a shallow bowl, cover and microwave at 30% power for 60 seconds, or until softened to the point of melting, but not yet melted. Combine butter and sugar in a medium sized mixing bowl. Beat until creamy (about 1-2 minutes). Add egg, vanilla and almond extract. Mix well. Combine flour and baking powder; gradually add to butter mixture with milk, beating until well combined.

2. Pack dough tightly into a spritz cookie press. Shape dough as desired, and place close together onto ungreased baking sheets. Bake 8-10 minutes, or until edges are lightly browned. Remove to wax paper lined wire racks to cool completely.

3. <u>Icing:</u> In a small saucepan over medium heat, stir together the butter and water until the butter melts. Remove from heat, and cool for 5 minutes. Add the sugar and food coloring to the butter mixture, and whisk vigorously until completely smooth and runny. As you work with the icing, it may thicken. Add more hot water, 1 teaspoon at a time, for creamy dipping consistency.

4. Line a baking sheet with wax paper. Place a wire rack over the wax paper. Use a fork to immerse each cookie in runny icing, and shake off excess. Place on wire rack (excess icing will drip onto wax paper), and immediately sprinkle with nonpareils. Let set (about 2 hours).

5. Store between sheets of wax paper in an airtight container at room temperature for up to 10 days, or in the refrigerator up to 3 weeks. Do not freeze.

1 1/2 Cups Soft Butter
1 Cup Superfine Sugar
1 Egg
1 Tsp. Vanilla
1/2 Tsp. Almond Extract
4 1/4 Cups Flour
1 Tsp. Baking Powder
1 Tbls. Milk

<u>Icing:</u>
1/2 Cup Soft Butter
4 Tbls. HOT Water
3 Cups Sifted Powdered Sugar
3 Drops Red Food Coloring
Multi Colored Nonpareils

Below 3,500 Feet
Oven: 350°
Flour: Subtract 1/4 Cup
Milk: Do Not Add Milk

tip

Superfine sugar blends and dissolves more quickly and evenly than granulated sugar. As a result, you get smoother texture, even browning and no graininess. It may be purchased in the baking section of your local supermarket.

tip

Butter should be very soft to incorporate properly into the recipe. Watch it soften in the microwave, and remove it when it appears on the verge of melting.

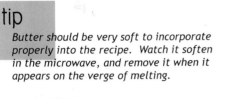
Variation

Add 1/4 Cup Unsweetened Cocoa Powder to Icing Ingredients to make a chocolate icing, or use a favorite food coloring to color the icing.

Caution

Do not chill the dough; it will crumble and fall apart.

Soft, old fashioned cookies
with a delightful pumpkin flavor!

1/2 Cup Soft Butter
1/2 Cup Butter Flavored
    Shortening
1/2 Cup Sugar
1 Egg
1/2 Cup Canned Pumpkin
1 Tsp. Vanilla
2 3/4 Cups Flour
2 Tsp. Pumpkin Pie Spice
1 Tsp. Baking Powder
1/2 Tsp. Salt
1/4 Cup Milk

Frosting:
6 oz. Soft Cream Cheese
4 Tbls. Soft Butter
1 Tsp. Vanilla
3 Cups Powdered Sugar
1/4 Cup Half n' Half
Finely Chopped Walnuts or
    Pecans

1. Combine butter, shortening and sugar in a large bowl. Beat at medium speed, scraping bowl often, until creamy. Add egg, pumpkin and vanilla; continue beating until mixed. Reduce speed to low and add remaining cookie ingredients until well mixed. Cover and chill dough 1 hour.

2. Preheat oven to 375°. Roll the dough with a floured mini rolling pin (see page 239) on a lightly floured surface, to 1/4 inch thickness. Always roll from the center to the edges. Cut the dough into shapes using floured 2" cookie cutters, cutting as close together as possible. Transfer dough to ungreased baking sheets, placing shapes 2 inches apart. Bake 8-10 minutes or until edges begin to brown. Transfer to wax paper lined wire racks to cool completely.

3. Frosting: Combine all ingredients except sugar and half n' half in a small bowl. Beat until creamy, scraping bowl often. Reduce speed to low, add powdered sugar and half n' half. Beat until smooth and creamy. Spread frosting on cookies and immediately sprinkle with nuts.

4. Store between sheets of wax paper in an airtight container in the refrigerator for up to 10 days. Unfrosted cookies keep 4 months in the freezer. Thaw at room temperature, then frost and decorate. Do not store cookies at room temperature.

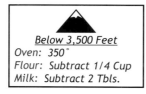

Below 3,500 Feet
Oven: 350°
Flour: Subtract 1/4 Cup
Milk: Subtract 2 Tbls.

tip

Toasting the nuts before chopping them enhances their flavor. To toast, arrange whole nuts in a single layer on a foil-lined baking sheet in a 350° oven for 8-10 minutes, stirring 2 or 3 times until desired flavor is reached. Cool completely before chopping.

tip

In a cookie recipe, shortening contributes to a softer-textured and more cake like cookie.

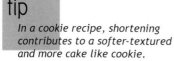
Variation

If you don't have pumpkin pie spice, combine 1 1/2 Tsp. Ground Cinnamon, 3/4 Tsp. Ground Ginger, 1/4 Tsp. Ground Nutmeg and 1/4 Tsp. Ground Cloves.

Low Sugar ✓ Favorite

The crisp texture and spicy taste of these holiday shaped cookies makes them the perfect treat alongside a steaming cup of hot chocolate or coffee.

1. Place flour, ginger, cinnamon, cardamom and cloves in a medium bowl; stir with a fork to combine, and set aside.

2. Beat brown sugar and butter in a large bowl until light and fluffy. Dissolve baking soda in hot water. Add to butter mixture. Gradually add flour mixture. Beat until dough forms. If dough is too crumbly, add more hot water, 1 tablespoon at a time, until dough holds together. Cover and refrigerate 1 hour.

3. Preheat oven to 375°. Grease baking sheets and set aside. Roll out dough on a lightly floured surface to 1/8 inch thickness. Cut dough with floured cookie cutters. Place cutouts 1 inch apart on prepared baking sheets. Bake 9-10 minutes or until firm and lightly browned. Remove cookies to wax paper lined wire racks to cool completely.

4. Royal Icing: Beat 1 room-temperature egg white until foamy. Gradually add sifted powdered sugar and almond extract; beating at low speed until moistened. Increase mixer speed to high and beat until icing is stiff. If necessary, add hot water, 1 teaspoon at a time, to thin, or 1/2 cup additional powdered sugar to thicken.

5. Store between sheets of wax paper in an airtight container at room temperature for up to 1 week, or in the refrigerator up to 10 days. Unfrosted cookies keep 6 months in your freezer. Thaw at room temperature, then frost and decorate.

2 Cups Flour
1 1/2 Tsp. Ground Ginger
1 1/2 Tsp. Cinnamon
1/2 Tsp. Ground Cardamom
1/2 Tsp. Ground Cloves
2/3 Cup Packed Brown Sugar
1/2 Cup Soft Butter
1/2 Tsp. Baking Soda
1/3 Cup Hot Water

Royal Icing:
1 Egg White at Room Temperature
2 Cups Sifted Powdered Sugar
1/2 Tsp. Almond Extract

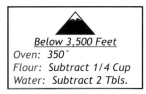
Below 3,500 Feet
Oven: 350°
Flour: Subtract 1/4 Cup
Water: Subtract 2 Tbls.

tip
A plastic squeeze bottle can be used for squeezing icing in patterns over cookies (see page 243). If the icing becomes too thick, microwave it inside the bottle for 15 second intervals at 30% power.

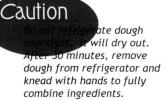

Caution
Do not refrigerate dough overnight. It will dry out. After 30 minutes, remove dough from refrigerator and knead with hands to fully combine ingredients.

√
Favorite

*Nuts, butter and a generous dusting
of powdered sugar garnish each tender cookie.*

1 1/4 Cups Soft Butter
1 Tsp. Vanilla
2 Cups Flour
1 1/3 Cups Finely Chopped
    Walnuts
2 Tbls. Powdered Sugar
1 Lb. Sifted Powdered Sugar

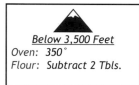

Below 3,500 Feet
Oven: 350˚
Flour: Subtract 2 Tbls.

tip

*Cookie dough will combine better if
butter is softened at least 2 hours at
room temperature, or, you can also
microwave butter for 30 seconds at
30% power.*

1. Preheat oven to 375˚. Use a nut mill to finely chop the
walnuts (see page 240). Place the powdered sugar in a shallow
bowl; set aside. In a large bowl, combine butter, vanilla, flour,
walnuts and 2 Tbls. powdered sugar. Beat until well combined
(about 2 minutes).

2. Use a large spoon, or your hands, to shape dough into
2 inch logs. Place 2 inches apart on ungreased baking sheets.
Bake 13-15 minutes, or until lightly browned on the bottoms.

3. Immediately transfer to wax paper lined wire racks. While
hot, roll cookies in powdered sugar 4 to 5 times until bright
white. Cool Completely. Roll in powdered sugar one more
time.

4. Store between sheets of wax paper in an airtight
container at room temperature for up to 1 week, or in the
refrigerator up to 10 days. Do not freeze.

Variation
*Substitute finely chopped
pecans for the walnuts.*

√
Favorite

*This centuries old cinnamon cookie recipe takes on
a new face with a nugget shape and cocoa laced topping.*

1. Preheat oven to 400˚. Spray baking sheets with nonstick cooking spray and set aside. Combine butter, shortening, sugar and egg in a medium sized mixing bowl. Beat 1 minute until well mixed. Stir in buttermilk and vanilla. Blend together flour, cinnamon, baking soda and salt. Add to mixture, and beat at medium speed until well combined. Cover and chill dough 30 minutes.

2. In a shallow bowl, combine topping ingredients and mix well. Shape dough into 1" diameter ropes. Cut into 1 inch pieces. Roll nuggets in topping mixture. Place 1 inch apart on prepared baking sheets. Sprinkle with additional topping, and bake 10-12 minutes or until set. Remove to wax paper lined wire racks to cool completely.

3. Store between sheets of wax paper in an airtight container at room temperature for up to 1 week, in the refrigerator up to 10 days, or in the freezer up to 4 months.

1/4 Cup Soft Butter
1/4 Cup Buttered Flavored
    Shortening
1 Cup Sugar
1 Egg
3/4 Cup Buttermilk
1 Tsp. Vanilla
2 1/4 Cups Flour
1/2 Tsp. Cinnamon
1/2 Tsp. Baking Soda
1/2 Tsp. Salt

<u>Topping:</u>
1/2 Cup Sugar
1 Tsp. Cinnamon
1 Tsp. Unsweetened Cocoa
    Powder

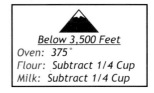

Below 3,500 Feet
Oven: 375˚
Flour: Subtract 1/4 Cup
Milk: Subtract 1/4 Cup

tip
*Chill the dough for 1 hour to
make it easier to handle.*

tip
*Shortening contributes to a
softer-texture and more cake
like cookie.*

These crisp little cookies have a hidden chocolate surprise inside!

1 Cup Soft Butter
1/2 Cup Powdered Sugar
1 Tsp. Vanilla
2 1/4 Cups Flour
1/2 Tsp. Salt
1/2 Cup Finely Chopped
    Walnuts
40 Milk Chocolate Kisses of all
    Varieties

Sugar Coating:
3 Cups Powdered Sugar
3 Tbls. Coarse Red Sugar
    (NO Substitutions)
3 Tbls. Coarse Green Sugar
    (NO Substitutions)

1. Preheat oven to 400˚. In a large bowl, beat the butter, powdered sugar and vanilla until well mixed (about 1 minute). On low speed, mix in flour, salt and walnuts. In a separate bowl, combine coating ingredients, mix well and set aside.

2. For each cookie, shape a measuring tablespoonful of dough around each chocolate kiss to form a 1-inch ball. Place 2 inches apart on ungreased baking sheets.

3. Bake 13-15 minutes, or until set and bottoms begin to turn golden brown. Immediately remove from baking sheets and roll in sugar coating. Cool completely on wax paper lined wire rack (about 20 minutes). Roll in sugar coating again.

4. Store between sheets of wax paper in an airtight container at room temperature for up to 1 week, or in the refrigerator up to 2 weeks. Do not freeze.

Below 3,500 Feet
Oven: 375˚
Flour: Subtract 1/4 Cup

tip

For test purposes, we used Hershey's Brand Chocolate Almond Kisses and Chocolate Caramel Kisses. Colored Coarse Sugars are found in the baking section of your local supermarket.

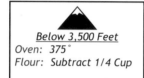

Variation

Experiment with the different flavored kisses.

Caution

Caramel Kisses will have a tendency to "leak" out during baking. Be sure to cover entire candy piece with dough.

These simple sweet treats are low in sugar and always a hit!

1. Preheat oven to 350˚. Line an 8-inch square baking pan with plastic food wrap, leaving a 2-inch overhang. Set aside.

2. Combine butter, sugar and almond extract in a medium bowl. Beat at medium speed, scraping bowl often, until creamy. Reduce speed to low; add flour and salt. Mix until well combined. Stir in chocolate chips and nonpareils.

3. Combine dough to form a ball, and knead 2 to 3 times. Pat dough evenly into prepared pan. Use a mini rolling pin (see page 239) to even out all edges and top. Cover and chill dough 30 minutes.

4. Use plastic wrap to lift dough from pan. With a sharp edge, cut dough into 8 rows, 8 cookies each row (64 total). Gently place squares 1/2 inch apart onto ungreased baking sheets. Bake 12-14 minutes or until bottoms are lightly browned. Cool completely on wax paper lined wire rack.

5. Store between sheets of wax paper in an airtight container at room temperature for up to 1 week, in the refrigerator up to 10 days, or freeze for up to 4 months.

1/2 Cup Plus 1 Tbls. Soft Butter
1/4 Cup Sugar
1/4 Tsp. Almond Extract
1 1/4 Cups Flour
1/4 Tsp. Salt
4 Tsp. Holiday Colored Nonpareils
1/3 Cup Miniature Semisweet Chocolate Chips

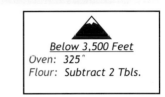

Below 3,500 Feet
Oven: 325˚
Flour: Subtract 2 Tbls.

tip

The dough contains no eggs, therefore, it can be made up to 1 week ahead, and covered tightly in plastic food wrap in the refrigerator until ready for use.

Caution
Do not over knead the dough; it will crumble and fall apart.

These Swedish paper thin cookies are butter rich, and full of almond and chocolate flavor!

✓ Favorite   Low Sugar

1 Cup Sliced Almonds
1/2 Cup Superfine Sugar
1/2 Cup Soft Butter
2 Tbls. Flour
1/2 Tsp. Salt
2 Tbls. Half n' Half
4 oz. Dark Chocolate

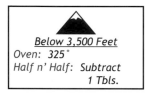

Below 3,500 Feet
Oven: 325°
Half n' Half: Subtract
                1 Tbls.

tip

Superfine sugar blends more quickly and evenly than granulated sugar. As a result, you get smoother texture, even browning and no graininess. It can be purchased in the Baking Section of your local supermarket.

tip

For test purposes, we used Hershey's Brand Special Dark Chocolate Bar.

1. Preheat oven to 350°. Lightly grease 2 baking sheets with nonstick cooking spray; set aside.

2. Place almonds in a resealable plastic bag and roll over several times with a rolling pin until very fine (i.e. no more visibly large pieces). Combine almonds, sugar, butter, flour, salt and half n' half in a heavy-based saucepan and mix well. Cook over medium heat until butter is melted and batter is smooth, stirring constantly. Remove from heat.

3. Drop batter by heaping teaspoonfuls, 3-4 inches apart (batter is runny and will spread), onto prepared baking sheets (you may only get 6-8 cookies per sheet). Bake 6-7 minutes, or until barely lightly browned at the edges, but bubbling in the center. Remove and let cookies sit on hot baking sheets 2 more minutes. Use a very thin spatula to remove to wax paper lined wire racks to cool completely.

4. Microwave the chocolate in a small microwave safe bowl at 60% power until melted (about 2-3 minutes). Transfer to a plastic squeeze bottle (see page 243) and drizzle over the tops of cookies. Let set (about 2 hours).

5. Do not cover chocolate until it has dried completely. Store between sheets of wax paper in an airtight tin, or foil covered container in a cool, dry place at room temperature for up to 1 week. Do not refrigerate or freeze.

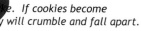

Caution

Do not overbake. If cookies become browned, they will crumble and fall apart.

Quick n' Easy   ✓ Favorite

Christmas Classics

Colorado Crater Cookies

Their odd appearance is deceiving; these cookies are butter rich, full of raspberry flavor, and best of all, made from refrigerated cookie dough!

1. Remove cookie dough from refrigerator and let sit at room temperature for about 1 hour. Use a nut mill to finely chop pecans (see page 240). Set aside in a small bowl. Spray a baking sheet with nonstick cooking spray and set aside.

2. Preheat oven to 375°. Lightly beat egg white in a small bowl until foamy. Add water and stir to combine. Shape dough into 1 inch balls and roll in egg white mixture, then in nuts. Place 2 inches apart on prepared baking sheet. Indent center of each cookie with your thumb, or the large end of a melon baller tool.

3. Bake 10-12 minutes or until edges are firm and lightly browned. Cookies may run together while baking (thus, their odd shape). Remove to wax paper lined wire racks. Immediately drop about 2 teaspoons preserves in dented center of each warm cookie. Use a knife to spread jam in a circle to create a "crater" look (see photo). When cookies have completely cooled, dust with powdered sugar.

4. Store between sheets of wax paper in an airtight container at room temperature for up to 1 week, or in the refrigerator up to 10 days. Do not freeze.

1 (16.5 oz.) Roll Refrigerated
    Sugar Cookie Dough
1 Beaten Egg White
1 Tbls. Water
1 Cup Finely Chopped Pecans
3/4 Cup Raspberry Preserves
Sifted Powdered Sugar

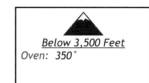
Below 3,500 Feet
Oven: 350°

Variation

Once you've made the first batch, try varying the flavor of jam to cherry, strawberry or even apricot. Substitute walnuts for the pecans.

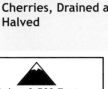

Favorite

*No one can resist the chewy coconut texture
in these cherry nut cookies!*

1 Cup Butter Flavored
   Shortening
1 Cup Sugar
1 Cup Packed Brown Sugar
2 Eggs
3/4 Tsp. Almond Extract
2 1/2 Cups Flour
1 Tsp. Baking Soda
1 Tsp. Salt
1/4 Cup Milk
2 1/2 Cups Sweetened Flaked
   Coconut
3/4 Cup Coarsely Chopped
   Almonds or Pecans
10 oz. Jar Maraschino
   Cherries, Drained and
   Halved

1. Preheat oven to 375˚. Combine shortening and sugars in a large mixing bowl. Beat until well mixed. Add eggs and almond extract and beat well.

2. Combine flour, baking soda and salt; gradually add to the creamed mixture, alternating with the milk, until mixture is smooth. Stir in coconut and nuts. Chill dough for at least 20 minutes.

3. Using a small cookie scoop (see page 239), drop dough by rounded scoopfuls 2 inches apart onto ungreased baking sheets. Press a cherry half in the center of each cookie. Bake 13-14 minutes or until lightly browned. Remove to wax paper lined wire racks to cool completely.

4. Store between sheets of wax paper in an airtight container at room temperature for up to 1 week, in the refrigerator up to 10 days, or in the freezer up to 4 months.

Below 3,500 Feet
Oven: 350˚
Flour: Subtract 1/4 Cup
Milk: Subtract 2 Tbls.

tip

*Coarsely chop nuts with a chef's knife
on a cutting board (see page 240).*

Caution

*If you fail to refrigerate the dough, the
cookies will spread too thin while baking.*

√
Favorite

*Choose firm, baking apples
for these sour cream cookie cakes.*

1. <u>Filling:</u> Melt Butter in a 2 quart saucepan. Stir in remaining filling ingredients, and mix well. Set aside. Preheat oven to 375°. Grease a 9 x 13 inch baking dish (glass only) with nonstick cooking spray and lightly dust with flour.

2. Combine Butter and sugar in a medium sized mixing bowl and beat until creamy (about 1 minute). Add eggs and vanilla and beat well. Combine all dry ingredients and add to mixture alternating with sour cream and milk. Mix until well combined.

3. Spread batter evenly into prepared pan. With a knife, mark off into 40 squares (8 rows by 5 rows). Place 1 teaspoon filling into the center of each square, and press into batter lightly. Bake 35-40 minutes, until a deep golden brown, and toothpick inserted in center comes out clean. Cool completely on a wire rack. Using a sharp knife, cut into 40 squares and place each inside a cupcake cup. Place on a large baking sheet.

4. <u>Icing:</u> Combine all ingredients except nuts, and beat well. Use a squeeze bottle to drizzle icing over cookie cakes. Immediately sprinkle with nuts. Let set (about 1 hour).

5. Store between sheets of wax paper in an airtight container in refrigerator for up to 10 days. Do not store at room temperature or freeze.

<u>Filling:</u>
4 Tbls. Soft Butter
1/2 Cup Packed Brown Sugar
1 Tbls. Flour
1 Tsp. Cinnamon
1/4 Tsp. Ground Nutmeg
1 Finely Chopped Apple
3/4 Cup Finely Chopped
   Walnuts

<u>Cake:</u>
2/3 Cup Soft Butter
1 Cup Sugar
2 Eggs
1 Tsp. Vanilla
2 1/4 Cups Flour
1/2 Tsp. Baking Powder
1/2 Tsp. Baking Soda
1/2 Tsp. Salt
1 Cup Sour Cream
1/4 Cup Milk

<u>Icing:</u>
1/4 Cup Melted Butter
1/2 Tsp. Vanilla
2 Cups Powdered Sugar
1/4 Cup Half n' Half
1/2 Cup Finely Chopped
   Walnuts

Paper Cupcake Cups

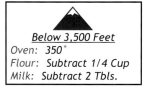

▲
Below 3,500 Feet
Oven: 350°
Flour: Subtract 1/4 Cup
Milk: Subtract 2 Tbls.

tip

For test purposes, we used a Granny Smith Apple. Other good baking apples are Rome, Jonathan, McIntosh, Braeburn, etc. Don't hesitate to leave the peel on the apple; it saves time, and adds nutrition.

Caution
Do not over beat the batter; dough will become tough.

Variation
Use finely chopped pecans in place of the walnuts.

40 Cookie Drops

✓ Favorite   Quick n' Easy

*Stir up Nana's timeless chocolate cookies in a jiffy --
they require no baking!*

1/2 Cup Soft Butter
1 3/4 Cup Sugar
1/3 Cup Unsweetened Cocoa
    Powder
2/3 Cup Half n' Half
    (No Substitutions)
1/2 Cup Creamy Peanut
    Butter
1 Tsp. Vanilla
2 3/4 Cups Quick Cooking
    Rolled Oats

1. Line baking sheets with wax paper; set aside. Melt butter in a 2 quart saucepan over medium heat. Add sugar, cocoa and half n' half. Stir constantly with a wooden spoon, and cook over medium high heat until mixture comes to a boil. Reduce heat to medium low and boil for exactly 1 minute, stirring occasionally. Remove from heat and stir in peanut butter and vanilla until melted.

2. Quickly add oatmeal and stir until well combined. Let batter sit 2 minutes. Using a small cookie scoop (see page 239), drop batter by heaping scoopfuls onto prepared baking sheets. Let cool completely (about 30 minutes).

3. Store between sheets of wax paper in an airtight container at room temperature for up to 1 week, or in the refrigerator up to 10 days. Do not freeze.

tip

To measure peanut butter, pour 1/2 cup water into a 1 cup sized measuring cup. Then, add peanut butter until the water line reaches the 1 cup line. Drain the water and add the peanut butter to the recipe.

tip

Work quickly to shape batter into cookies; otherwise dough may set up and lose it's shine.

Variation

Add 1/2 Cup Coarsely Chopped Peanuts or 3/4 Cup Candy Coated Mini Milk Chocolate Baking Bits to batter.

Caution

Do not boil mixture longer than 1 minute; it will burn easily.

Favorite

*This old world recipe is for a cookie so chocolatey rich --
thanks to the creamy, fudgy, ganache like filling!*

1. Preheat oven to 350°. Line baking sheets with parchment paper. Use a mini chopper to finely grind almonds. In a small measuring cup, stir together flour and cocoa; set aside.

2. In a large mixing bowl, beat butter, sugar and vanilla until light and fluffy, scraping sides of bowl often. Beat in almonds. Stir in flour mixture just until mixture is combined. Do NOT chill dough.

3. Using a small cookie scoop (see page 239), drop dough by scoopfuls 2 inches apart on prepared baking sheets. Flatten dough to 1/4 inch thickness with a glass bottom dipped in sugar. Bake 12-14 minutes or until firm. Leave cookies on hot baking sheets to cool completely.

4. <u>Filling:</u> Melt chocolate in a 1-quart oven proof saucepan using the oven method described on page 245. Carefully heat the whipping cream over medium low heat to lukewarm. Gradually add cream to chocolate, and stir until mixture is shiny and smooth. For each sandwich cookie, spread about 1 tablespoon filling onto bottom of 1 cookie; top with second cookie, and squeeze together gently until filling spreads out to edges of cookies. Let set (about 2 hours).

5. Store between sheets of wax paper in an airtight container at room temperature for 5 days, or in the refrigerator up to 10 days. Do not freeze.

2/3 Cup Flour
2 Tbls. Unsweetened Cocoa
    Powder
3/4 Cup Soft Butter
1 Cup Sugar
1 Tsp. Vanilla
1 1/2 Cups Finely Ground
    Almonds

<u>Filling:</u>
1/3 Cup Heavy Whipping
    Cream
8 oz. Milk Chocolate

tip

This cookie dough contains no eggs, so it may be made ahead and stored in a tightly covered container in the refrigerator for up to 1 week. Let sit at room temperature for 1 hour before baking as instructed.

Caution
Handle with care; cookies are very delicate and break easily.

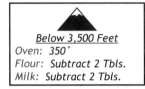
✓
Favorite

*Chocolate kisses - - an unbeatable sweetness
to compliment the peanut butter in these cookies!*

1/2 Cup Butter Flavored
      Shortening
1/2 Cup Creamy Peanut Butter
1/2 Cup Sugar
1/2 Cup Packed Brown Sugar
1 Tsp. Baking Powder
1/4 Tsp. Baking Soda
1 Egg
1/4 Cup Milk
1 Tsp. Vanilla
1 3/4 Cups Flour
1/4 Cup Sugar
Milk Chocolate Kisses

1. Preheat oven to 375°. In a large mixing bowl, beat shortening and peanut butter 30 seconds. Add the sugars, baking powder and baking soda. Beat until combined, scraping sides of bowl often. Add the egg, milk and vanilla and beat well. Beat in as much of the flour as you can with the mixer. Add any remaining flour, and stir just until combined. Cover dough and refrigerate for 1 hour.

2. Using a small cookie scoop (see page 239), form dough into 1 inch balls. Roll in 1/4 cup sugar and place 2 inches apart onto ungreased baking sheets. Bake 12-14 minutes or until edges are firm and bottoms are lightly browned. Immediately press a chocolate kiss into center of each hot cookie. Transfer to wax paper lined wire racks to cool completely.

3. Store between sheets of wax paper in an airtight container at room temperature for up to 1 week, in the refrigerator up to 10 days or in the freezer up to 4 months.

Below 3,500 Feet
Oven: 350°
Flour: Subtract 2 Tbls.
Milk: Subtract 2 Tbls.

---

tip

To measure peanut butter, pour 1/2 cup water into a 1 cup sized measuring cup. Add peanut butter until the water line reaches the 1 cup level. Drain the water and add the peanut butter to the recipe.

tip

For test purposes, we used Hershey's Brand Milk Chocolate Kisses.

Kittredge Macaroon Kisses

√
Favorite

*These out-of-this-world chewy cookies combine coconut and chocolate,
laced with almond flavoring.*

1. In a large mixing bowl, cream butter, cream cheese and sugar until light and fluffy (about 1 minute). Add egg yolk and almond extract and beat well. Combine flour, baking powder and salt; gradually add to creamed mixture. Stir in 3 cups of the coconut. Cover dough tightly with plastic wrap, and chill 1 hour.

2. Preheat oven to 375˚. Using a small cookie scoop (see page 239), shape dough into balls and roll in remaining coconut. Place 2 inches apart on ungreased baking sheets. Bake 12-14 minutes or until lightly browned. Remove from oven; immediately press unwrapped kiss into top of each hot cookie. Let sit on hot baking sheet 1 more minute. Remove to wax paper lined wire racks to cool completely.

3. Store between sheets of wax paper in an airtight container at room temperature for up to 3 days, or in the refrigerator up to 1 week. Do not freeze.

1/3 Cup Soft Butter
4 oz. Soft Cream Cheese
3/4 Cup Sugar
1 Egg Yolk
2 Tsp. Almond Extract
1 1/3 Cups Flour
2 Tsp. Baking Powder
1/2 Tsp. Salt
14 oz. Pkg. Sweetened
**   Flaked Coconut, Divided**
48 Milk Chocolate Kisses

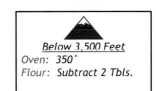

Below 3,500 Feet
Oven: 350˚
Flour: Subtract 2 Tbls.

Caution
*Do not freeze macaroon batter;
the cookies will not bake
properly.*

tip
*For test purposes, we
used Hershey's Brand Milk
Chocolate Kisses.*

6 Dozen Cookies

Quick n' Easy   Favorite

The texture and taste of this holiday chocolate chip cookie will delight you!

1/2 Cup Soft Butter
1/2 Cup Shortening
1 1/4 Cups Packed Brown
    Sugar
3/4 Tsp. Baking Soda
1/4 Tsp. Salt
3 Eggs
2 Tsp. Vanilla
1/4 Cup Milk
3 1/2 Cups Flour
1 Cup Candy Coated Miniature
    Milk Chocolate Baking Bits
1 Cup Chopped Pecans

Below 3,500 Feet
Oven: 350˚
Flour: Subtract 1/4 Cup
Milk: Subtract 2 Tbls.

1. Preheat oven to 375˚. In a large mixing bowl, beat butter and shortening on medium speed for 30 seconds. Add brown sugar, baking soda, and salt; beat until light and fluffy. Add eggs and vanilla; beat well.

2. Add milk and flour, and mix at low speed, just until combined. Stir in chocolate bits and nuts.

3. Using a small cookie scoop (see page 239), drop batter by rounded scoopfuls 2 inches apart onto ungreased baking sheets.

4. Bake 13-14 minutes or until golden. Remove to wax paper lined wire racks to cool completely.

5. Store between sheets of wax paper in an airtight container at room temperature for up to 1 week, in the refrigerator up to 2 weeks, or freeze for up to 4 months.

tip

For testing purposes, we used M&M's Brand Mini Baking Bits.

tip

You can freeze the dough balls; just shape dough into balls on a foil lined baking sheet. Freeze until firm (about 2 hours). Then, transfer to a freezer resealable plastic bag. Bake frozen cookie balls, adding a few minutes to the baking time.

Low Sugar

☑ Favorite

Cream cheese is the secret ingredient to creating these soft, flaky, pastry cookies with a rich flavored fruit filling.

1. Grease baking sheets with nonstick cooking spray and set aside. Combine butter and cream cheese in a large mixing bowl. Beat at medium speed until well combined (about 1 minute). Reduce speed to low, and add flour and salt. Mix until well combined. Cover and chill dough 1 hour.

2. Preheat oven to 375˚. Beat egg white and water in a small mixing bowl until frothy. Place coarse sugar in a shallow bowl. Use a small cookie scoop (see page 239) to shape dough into 1 inch balls. Roll dough in egg mixture, and then coarse sugar. Place 2 inches apart on prepared baking sheets. Using your thumb, or the small end of a melon baller tool, create an indent in the center of each cookie. Spoon about 1/2 scant teaspoon cherry preserves into center of each cookie. Bake 22-24 minutes, or until edges are golden brown. Transfer to wax paper lined wire racks to cool completely.

3. Store between sheets of wax paper in an airtight container at room temperature for up to 5 days, or in the refrigerator up to 2 weeks. Do not freeze.

1 Cup Soft Butter
8 oz. Soft Cream Cheese
2 1/4 Cups Flour
1/2 Tsp. Salt
1 Beaten Egg White
1 Tbls. Water
Coarse Red and White Sugar
Cherry Preserves

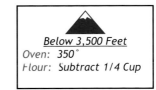

Below 3,500 Feet
Oven: 350˚
Flour: Subtract 1/4 Cup

Variation

Substitute your favorite fruit preserve.

Essential Kitchen Ingredients

Spending a little more on key ingredients, will pay off big time, in the rave reviews of your baked goods and candies.

Butter (Salted or Unsalted)
Butter is preferred in all our recipes. The flavor is far superior to margarine, and the cost differential is not that great.

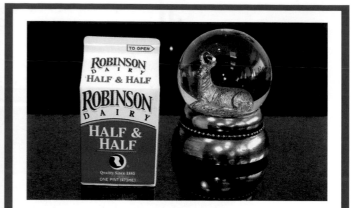

Half n' Half
An absolute MUST for melting caramels.
Contributes to a creamier candy and richer tasting baked good.

Brand Names
Don't skimp with store brands. Buy the real thing.
Everyone will notice a difference in texture and taste!

Food Coloring
You'll get the best results due to ease in measuring and color consistency.

Lining Pans with Aluminum Foil
Invert the pan, and shape the foil over the bottom.
Lift the shaped foil off, and fit it into the upright pan.

Nonstick Cooking Spray
A quick and flawless way to grease pans.
Lightly dust with flour for added protection.

The proper cooking tools are essential for creating baked goods and candies with a professional look and taste. Most tools can be purchased at discount stores.

Baking Sheet
Cookies bake more evenly on sheets that have raised edges as shown.

Wire Rack
Set a hot pan on top to cool readily. Line with wax paper and cool baked cookies.

Cookie Scoops
Available in small and large sizes. Assures uniformity in size of all cookies and candies.

Thin Spatulas
For ease in removing baked goods from hot cookie sheets, and ideal for lifting bars and candies from a baking pan.

Pastry Blender
Used for cutting butter or shortening into small pieces while incorporating into flour for cookie and bar doughs.

Mini Rolling Pin
Invaluable for evenly spreading out dough in pans, and rolling small quantities of dough for cookie cutting. Hand wash.

Essential Kitchen Tools

The proper cooking tools are essential for creating baked goods and candies with a professional look and taste. Most tools can be purchased at discount stores.

Nut Mill
Used to finely chop soft nuts like walnuts and pecans. NOT for peanuts, almonds, etc. Hand wash blade section.

Chef's Knife and Cutting Board
Used to finely or coarsely chop all types of nuts. Hand wash knife.

Nut Choppers
Used to coarsely or finely chop hard nuts like almonds, peanuts, hazelnuts, etc. Will also finely chop hard peppermint candy.

Chop Nuts in a Resealable Bag
To crush nuts, place in a resealable plastic bag and roll over several times with a rolling pin for desired sized pieces.

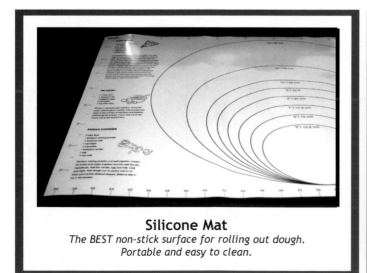

Silicone Mat
The BEST non-stick surface for rolling out dough. Portable and easy to clean.

Pastry Brushes
Used to apply melted butter or glazes to cookies, and evenly spread jams and jellies as bar toppings.

Wooden Spoons
*Essential in candy making, since the
handles don't get hot.*

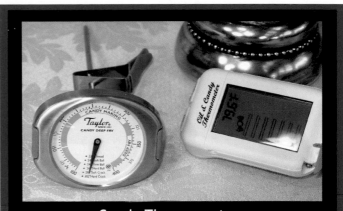

Candy Thermometers
*Invest in the "Taylor" Brand, with a stainless steel back,
and a clip to attach to the cooking pan.
The digital model is unbelievably accurate, guaranteeing success.*

Timer
*Handy when the recipe calls for a quick timing,
or when baking 2 cookie batches simultaneously.*

Kitchen Shears
*Helpful for cutting sticky or soft items
like whole marshmallows or caramels.*

Treat Bags with Ties
*Wonderful for packaging popcorn and nuts for gift giving.
Available at discount stores.*

Cookie Cutters and Press
*The variety of designs and size, enhances the
creative cook's ability to bake up works of art!*

Essential Kitchen Tools

The proper cooking tools are essential for creating baked goods and candies with a professional look and taste. Most tools can be purchased at discount stores.

Ovenproof Saucepans
Exclusively for chocolate. We prefer stainless steel with long handles. Dishwasher safe.

Heavy Saucepans
Essential for candy making. We prefer the dark coated nonstick. Stock up on 1, 2 , 3 and 4-quart sizes.

Dark Coated Baking Pans
Do NOT use at any time for baking. They absorb more heat, and affect moisture and browning.

Powdered Sugar and Cocoa Sifters
Prevents powdered sugar and cocoa from clumping while it's being sprinkled onto cookies and bars.

Parchment Paper
Excellent nonstick surface for cookie baking and candy making. Especially handy when dipping chocolates.

Spreaders
A must have for the professional look when spreading frostings, fudge layers and brownie batters in the pan.

Sharp Edge
Commonly known as a "dough scraper", used to evenly cut soft baked goods and candies like brownies, bars and fudges.

Cleaver
Used to evenly cut hard candies, brittles, almond bark, some fudges, and chocolate. Available at specialty kitchen stores.

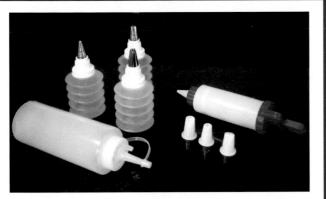

Decorator Tools and Squeeze Bottles
We prefer squeeze bottles, syringe sets, and bottles with decorative tips over the traditional messy bags with tips.

Airtight Storage Containers
The airtight lids keep cookies soft and baked goods fresh at room temperature, or in the refrigerator and freezer.

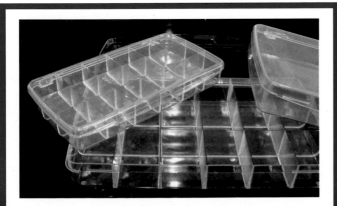

Plastic Storage Boxes
Keep homemade chocolates candy store fresh. Found in the craft section of local discount and craft supply stores.

Chocolate Storage Containers
Airtight tins and boxes are excellent, because they protect the chocolate from odor absorption and moisture.

Melting and Dipping Chocolate

Tools For Melting and Dipping Chocolate

Photo below illustrates common tools for the process of making beautifully dipped chocolates.
Dipping tools are common mesh strainers, spatulas or tongs. If you bend the handles in a perpendicular position,
they become excellent chocolate dipping tools.

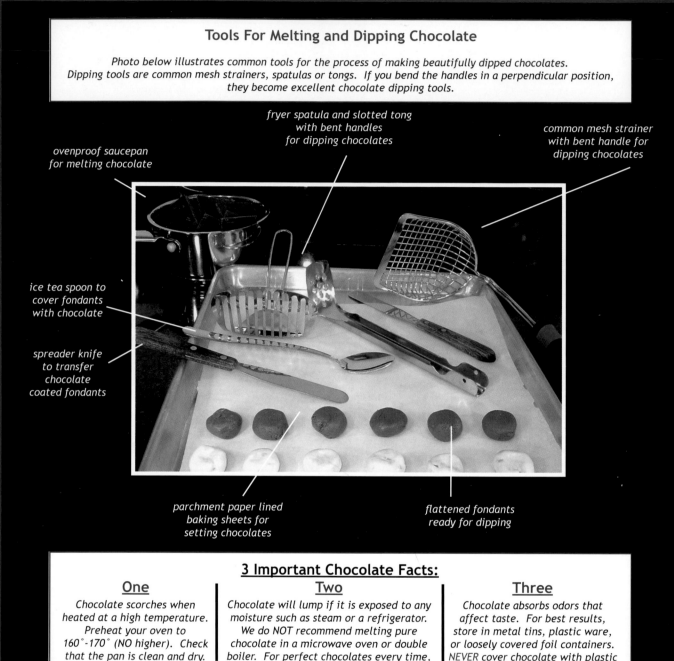

fryer spatula and slotted tong
with bent handles
for dipping chocolates

common mesh strainer
with bent handle for
dipping chocolates

ovenproof saucepan
for melting chocolate

ice tea spoon to
cover fondants
with chocolate

spreader knife
to transfer
chocolate
coated fondants

parchment paper lined
baking sheets for
setting chocolates

flattened fondants
ready for dipping

3 Important Chocolate Facts:

One
Chocolate scorches when heated at a high temperature. Preheat your oven to 160°-170° (NO higher). Check that the pan is clean and dry. All recipes in the book use chocolate bars that can easily be broken into 2 oz. pieces for melting.

Two
Chocolate will lump if it is exposed to any moisture such as steam or a refrigerator. We do NOT recommend melting pure chocolate in a microwave oven or double boiler. For perfect chocolates every time, use the oven melting method.
NEVER coat centers that are cold or frozen; the chocolate will discolor or lump.
NEVER add anything like paraffin, or oil to the chocolate; it will ruin the taste!

Three
Chocolate absorbs odors that affect taste. For best results, store in metal tins, plastic ware, or loosely covered foil containers. NEVER cover chocolate with plastic wrap, or store in a plastic airtight container. Store in a cool, dry, place (closed kitchen cabinet is perfect), away from sunlight. sunlight, and strong odors.

Amount to Melt: *Figure out how many pounds of finished chocolates you want, and melt HALF the amount in chocolate (if you want 5 pounds of finished chocolates, melt 2 1/2 pounds of chocolate).*

Shelf Life: *Purchased chocolate bars will stay fresh for about 1 year if kept in a cool, dry place.*

Freezing: *To freeze, wrap in moisture and vapor proof paper or heavy foil. Check that it is airtight, or moisture will seep in and ruin the chocolate.*

Oven Proof Saucepan

Break up chocolate and place in an oven proof saucepan.
If melting up to 16 oz., use a 1-quart size and melt 30 minutes.
If melting over 16 oz., use a 2-quart size and melt 40 minutes.

Melt Uncovered at 160° - 170°

Do NOT melt at a higher temperature. Chocolate can sit in
the oven up to 45 minutes at this temperature. If chocolate
becomes too thick, return to oven for 15 minutes.

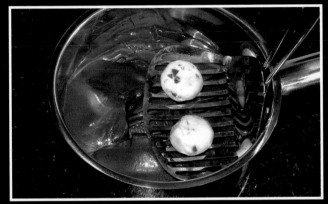

Dip Centers into Chocolate

Use a pot holder to remove pan from oven (handle is HOT).
Place centers on your favorite dipping tool (see previous page),
and lower into chocolate until tool rests on bottom of pan.

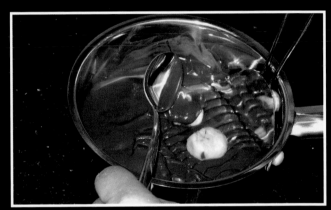

Use Spoon to Cover

Use an ice tea spoon (see previous page),
to gently cover entire candy with chocolate.
If necessary, gently stir the chocolate, however, do NOT
over stir; it will clump, harden, and lose it's shine.

Shake Off Excess

Lift dipping tool and covered candies out of the pan,
and gently shake off excess chocolate.

Let Set 2 Hours

Use a spreader knife (see previous page) to transfer
dipped candies onto paper lined baking sheets to set.
Chocolate will set in about 2 hours (away from sunlight).

The Candy Thermometer Test

Why You MUST Perform This Test:

Water boils at about 212°F at SEA LEVEL and decreases approximately 2°F for each 1000 feet rise in altitude. Therefore, if you live at 5000 feet, water will boil at about 202°F. In candy making, the thermometer tells you how much water has boiled out of the sugar solution. If water boils at a lower temperature at your altitude, the water is boiling out of the candy mixture at a lower temperature. This means that your candy will actually reach the proper cooked stage at a lower temperature. All the candy recipes in this cookbook are written for sea level, and must be adjusted to your altitude. Regardless of the altitude at which you live, test your thermometer in boiling water, and write down the boiling point (third column from right below). Then, according to your calculations in the chart below, adjust the temperature to cook candy for each recipe at your altitude.

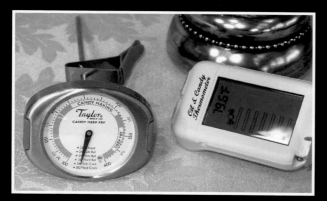

Purchase the Right Thermometer

Invest in the "Taylor" Brand, with a stainless steel back, and a clip to attach to the cooking pan. We prefer the digital type (right in photo); it is foolproof, and results in the perfect candy every time!

Test in Boiling Water

A thermometer needs to be tested before its initial use, and every year thereafter. To do this, place the thermometer in at least 2 inches of water. Bring the water to a boil, and let the water boil for 5 minutes. Read the temperature at eye level (if you look down, the temperature will appear to be lower than it actually is). Note the temperature below (see chart) at which the water boils at your altitude. It should be between 200-212°F.

Date of Test	212°F	Boiling Point	Subtract Boiling Point From 212°F
12/1/08	212°F	202°	*Subtract 10°*
	212°F		*Subtract ____*
	212°F		*Subtract ____*
	212°F		*Subtract ____*
	212°F		*Subtract ____*

In the example, when testing the thermometer, water boiled at 202°F. If a recipe calls for cooking to 238°F, you would subtract 10° (212°F minus 202°F; or 10 degrees) and cook to 228°F.

For best results, we recommend you replace your candy thermometer every 5 years.

Choose a LOW Humidity Day

1. *Use butter. It will always result in a better taste and texture.*
2. *Invest in Brand Name ingredients. Candies will look and taste like they were purchased at a candy store.*
3. *Always make candy on a DRY day (if humidity is higher than 60%, you risk failure with the recipes).*
   For best results, ingredients should be at or near room temperature. Remove from refrigerator
   30 minutes before starting. Always assemble ingredients together BEFORE you start to cook, then put
   them aside as you use them. That way, you'll never forget an ingredient or include it twice. You DON'T
   want to be measuring ingredients, when you SHOULD be stirring the candy mixture.

Add Liquids First

1. *To keep candy from burning, use a heavy saucepan (left photo), or one that's lined with a dark nonstick*
   material (right photo). It should be 6-7 inches in diameter, and have a straight, not slanted side, so a
   candy thermometer can be clipped on easily.
2. *Use wooden spoons in all candy recipes. The handles won't get HOT while your stirring constantly.*
3. *ALWAYS place the liquids in the pan first, then the sugars. This will eliminate sugar crystals from forming on*
   the inside of the cooking pan. If sugar crystals become present, wipe down the insides of the pan with
   a damp paper towel. After initially stirring a mixture to dissolve the sugar, be sure that the spoon is
   thoroughly rinsed, before returning it to the pan for additional stirring. Even a SINGLE sugar granule
   on the spoon, can cause a chain reaction, and the entire batch of candy can develop a grainy texture.

Hard Candies
They absorb moisture.
A glass jar with lid is perfect.
NEVER store in the
refrigerator.

All Candies
To prevent candies from exchanging flavors,
always store different types of candy in
separate containers, using wax paper between
layers. Keep hard candy and soft candy in
different containers, to avoid
moisture absorption.

Chocolates
Keep homemade chocolates candy
store fresh, in these hard
plastic containers with small
compartments. Store in a cool, dry,
dark place (closed kitchen cabinet
away from direct sunlight).

Recipe Category Index

This index lists every recipe by common terminology, as well as helpful tips, tools and techniques.

Recipe Ingredient Index
This index lists recipes by favorite ingredient.

Almond Bark
Allenspark Marbled Mint Bark, 154
Bedrock Bark, 79
Breckenridge Bark, 99
Carson's Cranberry Crackles, 117
Catamount Crunch, 109
Delta Cream Fudgits, 41
Garden City Glacier Candy, 120
Jesse's Double Decker Minties, 152
Popo's Peanut Fudge, 56
Virginia City Truffles, 69
Perron's Peanut Clusters, 36
Powderhorn Penouche, 20
Ruthie's Cookie Bones for Dogs, 211
Carson City Snack Mix, 103
Minty Mountain Truffles, 70
Sno Mountain Ranch Pretzels, 107
State Fair Fudge, 59
Windsor's Peppermint Nougats, 144

Almond Extract
Scobey's Almond Twixies, 182
Bow Mar Bonbons, 21
Carissa's Chewies, 207
Cherry Chocolate Biscotti, 126
Durango Spice Cookies, 217
Fall River Fondant Variations, 43
Kittredge Macaroon Kisses, 233
Lyon's Cherry Almond Chews, 224
Mountain Cream Candy Logs, 25
Payette Party Peak Cookies, 226
Pocatello Pine Nut Drops, 186
Riggins Raspberry Drops, 202
Steamboat Spritz, 215
Tabernash Tidbits, 221

Cake Mix or Brownie Mix
Bridlegate Brownies, 162
Black Eagle Brownie Bars, 164
Kootenai Kandy Bars, 177
Paonia Peanut Bars, 178
Kalispell Kabinet Kandy, 47
Twin Lakes Treasure Bars, 167

Candy Bars
Bear Lake Bridge Mix, 78
Briggsdale Popcorn Nougats, 106
Bozeman Buckthorn Cookies, 190
Boulder City Celebrity Fudge, 52
Gore Range Bars, 160
Kim's Caramel Fudge, 55
Marlene's Magic Mint Fudge, 135
Kalispell Kabinet Kandy, 47

Candy Bars, Mint
Heidi's Hidden Minties, 147
Idledale Minties, 140
Manitou Mint Squares, 149
Manor House Truffles, 134

Moffat's Mint Drizzles, 139

Caramel
Cedar City Pattie Candy, 20
Bailey's Brownies, 161
Boulder Bites, 13
Bunny's Brittle Bars, 87
Coal Creek Cracker Turtles, 116
Como's Caramel Cluster
    Creams, 30
Cooper's Crunch Bites, 113
Frederick's Chocolate
    Potato Chips, 39
Glen Haven Candies, 119
Gunnison's Grizzly Candy, 38
Jefferson's Turtle Dip Cookies, 191
Kootenai Kandy Bars, 177
Monarch's Mistletoe Candy, 31
Mountain Cream Candy Logs, 25
Nonie's Crunchy Candy
    Bundles, 108

Cereal, Breakfast
Crispy Rice
Carson's Cranberry Crackles, 117
Black Eagle Brownie Bars, 164
Conejos Cherry Crinkles, 125
Decker's Double Crispies, 118
Garden City Glacier Candy, 120
Glen Haven Candies, 119
Meeker's Mint Macaroons, 145
Nonie's Crunchy Candy
    Bundles, 108
Paonia Peanut Bars, 178
Perron's Peanut Clusters, 36
Ricky's Crunch Candy, 121
Granola
Virginia City Truffles, 69
Penrose Partridge Bars, 124
Oatmeal
Cherry Hills Chocolate Royals, 165
Glendale Coconut Cobbler Bars, 173
Gore Range Bars, 160
Glenrock's Granny Apple Squares, 176
Larkspur Lemon Bars, 175
Redstone Twinkle Bars, 172
Wiggin's Cocoa No-Bakes, 230
Other
Carson City Snack Mix, 103
Vail Valley Snowflake
    Crunchers, 123

Chips, Baking
Butterscotch Flavored
Buffalo Crunch Candy, 37
Cotopaxi Candy Cups, 34
Dakota Dream Bars, 179
Rawlins Eagle's Nest Candy, 35
Gore Range Bars, 160

Chips, Baking
Butterscotch Flavored
Gunnison's Grizzly Candy, 38
Hartzel's Maple Nut Creams, 23
Kim's Caramel Fudge, 55
Timnath Taffy, 11
Cherry Flavored
Mimi's Cherry Puff Candy, 33
Cinnamon Flavored
Billings Biscotti, 127
Payette Party Peak Cookies, 226
Milk Chocolate
Best of the West Toffee, 8
Bozeman Buckthorn Cookies, 190
Bunny's Brittle Bars, 87
Gunnison's Grizzly Candy, 38
Twin Peaks Truffles, 66
Mint Flavored
Delta Cream Fudgits, 41
Missoula Mint Rounds, 141
Palisade Peppermint Tidbits, 150
Pinehurst Peppermint Sticks, 142
Minty Mountain Truffles, 70
Peanut Butter Flavored
Bridlegate Brownies, 162
Paonia Peanut Bars, 178
Premium White
Buffalo Crunch Candy, 37
Drew's Peanut Butter Creams, 19
Lolo's Nutty Crunch Bars, 88
Redstone Twinkle Bars, 172
Vail Valley Snowflake
    Crunchers, 123
Semisweet Chocolate
Bailey's Brownies, 161
Baker Mountain Biscotti, 128
Berthoud Biscotti, 129
Bridlegate Brownies, 162
Byers Cream Cheese Truffles, 65
Custer's Candy Cane Bon Bons, 138
Carissa's Chewies, 207
Carson's Cranberry Crackles, 117
Boulder City Celebrity Fudge, 52
Cherry Chocolate Biscotti, 126
Cherry Hills Chocolate Royals, 165
Black Eagle Brownie Bars, 164
Conejos Cherry Crinkles, 125
Logandale Fudge Bites, 62
Rawlins Eagle's Nest Candy, 35
Fox Run Fudge, 54
Gore Range Bars, 160
Idaho Falls Confetti Fudge, 64
Holly's Cinnamon Swirlies, 205
Holyoke Log Cookies, 208
Jesse's Double Decker Minties, 152
Kim's Caramel Fudge, 55

Cook's Notes